THE READY RESOURCE FOR

Relief Society

—AND—

MELCHIZEDEK PRIESTHOOD

2018 CURRICULUM

Also by
TRINA BOICE

Base Hits and Home Run Relationships:
What Women Wish Guys Knew

My Future's So Bright, I Gotta Wear Shades

Bright Ideas for Young Women Leaders

Easy Enrichment Ideas:
Thinking Outside the Green Gelatin Box

Dad's Night: Fantastic Family Nights in 5 Minutes

Ready Resource for Relief Society:
2010, 2011, 2012, 2013, 2014, 2015, 2016, 2017

Sabbath Solutions: More Than 350 Ways
You Can Worship on the Lord's Day

Climbing Family Trees: Whispers in the Leaves

Great Ideas for Primary Activity Days

Parties with aA Purpose:
Exciting Ideas for Ward Activities

Primarily for Cub Scouts

How to Stay UP in a DOWN Economy

You're What? 103 Creative Ways to
Announce Your Pregnancy

A Gift of Love—A Visual Pun Book of the Heart

THE READY
RESOURCE FOR

Relief Society

— AND —

MELCHIZEDEK
PRIESTHOOD

2018 CURRICULUM

{ TRINA BOICE }

CFI
AN IMPRINT OF CEDAR FORT, INC.
SPRINGVILLE, UTAH

This is not an official publication of The Church of Jesus Christ of Latter-day Saints. The opinions and views expressed herein belong solely to the author and do not necessarily represent the opinions or views of Cedar Fort, Inc. Permission for the use of sources, graphics, and photos is also solely the responsibility of the author.

ISBN 13: 978-1-4621-2104-5

Published by CFI, an imprint of Cedar Fort, Inc.
2373 W. 700 S., Springville, UT 84663
Distributed by Cedar Fort, Inc., www.cedarfort.com

Library of Congress Control Number: 2017957421

Cover design by Shawnda T. Craig
Cover design © 2018 by Cedar Fort, Inc.
Edited by Melissa Caldwell
Typeset by Kaitlin Barwick

Printed in the United States of America

10 9 8 7 6 5 4 3 2 1

Printed on acid-free paper

Contents

FIRST SUNDAY:
COUNSELING TOGETHER ABOUT LOCAL NEEDS

SECOND & THIRD SUNDAYS:
GENERAL CONFERENCE MESSAGES

FOURTH SUNDAY:
SPECIAL TOPICS CHOSEN BY
GENERAL CHURCH LEADERS

FIFTH SUNDAY:
TOPICS CHOSEN BY THE BISHOPRIC

Acknowledgments

I want to thank Cedar Fort Publishing for inviting me to share this annual adventure with them! I also want to send a big thank-you to Katy Watkins, Jessica Romrell, and Shawnda Craig, for all of their help with this edition.

A special thanks goes to my wonderfully supportive family for taking care of everything around me while I was busy pounding away at my computer keyboard. My husband and four sons inspire me to try harder and be better every day. I'm also forever grateful for my extended family's continued enthusiastic support, unconditional love, and kind encouragement.

Thank you to all the faithful members of the Church who valiantly magnify their callings and give of their time and talents to bless those around them. Heavenly Father knows that when we teach others, we learn more deeply ourselves. They say that God loves all people, but especially teachers, because they remind Him of His Son!

Not only should we read the scriptures and have a meaningful gospel study plan, but we're also commanded to FEAST on the scriptures! It is my hope that this book serves as a helpful utensil to enjoy your meal!

Introduction

The format for the 2018 lessons in Relief Society and priesthood quorums is completely unique and an exciting change! The new changes reflect a desire to ensure that teachers are meeting the specific needs of their wards and branches. The Savior taught us that conversion occurs one by one; therefore, our lessons need to be more carefully tailored to those who attend our classes and to the communities in which we live.

This resource handbook will follow the same structure that the First Presidency has announced for the 2018 lesson formats:

- **First Sunday:** Counseling together for local needs
- **Second and Third Sundays:** General Conference messages
- **Fourth Sunday:** Special topic chosen by general Church leaders
- **Fifth Sunday:** Topic chosen by the bishopric

The topic until the next general conference will be the Sabbath day, and the other topics included in this resource have been prayerfully chosen as a guide for the rest of the year. Church leaders have talked about these topics a lot in recent years. They are the topics that we, as members of the Church, seem to struggle with the most and the ones that pertain to our growth the most in these latter days. *Always follow the direction of your local leaders when different topics are given to you.*

The *Ready Resource for Relief Society and Melchizedek Priesthood* for 2018 is designed to be a helpful, inspiring resource to make lesson preparation easier, allowing teachers more time to carefully create an experience that meets the needs of their unique ward or branch. Because the Church is growing rapidly and Saints are gathered across the globe, teachers will need to prayerfully consider the material that will be taught each week, focusing on the individuals in their class. The emphasis should be on ENGAGING classes and quorums in discussions, rather than showcasing a teacher who does all of the talking. The more included people feel during a lesson, the more they will return to their homes edified and motivated to APPLY what they have learned.

The gospel means "good news" and should bring us great joy! Members of The Church of Jesus Christ of Latter-day Saints should be the happiest people around. May you feel the Savior's loving arms enfold you as you teach your dear sisters and brothers and feed His sheep.

Each chapter includes hymns appropriate for the lesson, quick summaries of the lesson material, quotes to supplement your class discussions, suggested artwork to display during your presentation, and object lessons to add pizzazz to your student participation. The weekly "Challenge" is a feature to encourage your students to immediately apply what they learn during your lesson. Two other teaching tools to strengthen spiritual growth and family relationships are the Seminary Scripture Mastery verses (perfect for parents of teens), and correlating topics in the Church's *Preach My Gospel* missionary manual (perfect for parents of future and current missionaries). You're not teaching lessons—you're teaching your brothers and sisters!

In addition, each chapter contains a space to take personal notes and record inspiration as you prepare your thoughts.

The most important tool is the Holy Ghost, which will help you know how to tailor each lesson to meet the needs of your class members.

Teaching with the Holy Ghost is THE MOST IMPORTANT tool in your class. Pray for the Holy Ghost to guide your study preparation before your lesson and for inspiration during your lesson. As you live the commandments and do your utmost to magnify your calling, you will receive personal revelation and direction on how you should share the lessons with your sisters and brothers.

The best lessons are not lectures, but rather, discussions where everyone participates. Try to involve the brothers and sisters in your class, encouraging them to share their experiences and testimonies of the principles you are teaching. They should leave your class feeling edified, enriched, and excited to live the gospel with joy!

Integrating various learning styles into your lessons improves retention and attention, assists in lesson planning, and inspires participants. Everyone learns differently, so be sure to include lots of variety in your teaching techniques. Try using some of the following ideas during your lessons:

STUDENT CENTERED

- Assignments
- Brainstorming
- Case Study
- Discussion

- Instructional Games
- Memorizing
- Note Taking
- Oral Reading

- Role-Playing
- Testimonies
- Debate
- Field Trip
- Games
- Panels
- Questions
- Class Journal
- Open-Ended Story
- Songs
- Crafts
- Worksheets

TEACHER CENTERED

- Jokes & Puns
- Lecture
- Oral Reading
- Storytelling
- Summarizing
- Guest Speaker
- Personal Photos & Videos
- Demonstration
- Surveys
- Catch Phrases & Tag Lines
- Questions
- Personal Emails
- Dramatization
- Feedback

MATERIALS CENTERED

- Bulletin Board
- Chalkboard
- Charts & Maps
- Displays
- Flash Cards
- Flannel Board
- DVD
- Flip Chart
- Overhead Transparency
- Pictures & Artwork
- Posters
- Puppet Show
- Dramatization
- Social Media
- Handouts
- Quizzes & Tests
- eBooks
- Mobile Apps
- Graphs
- Original Films
- Artwork
- Comics
- PowerPoint Presentations
- Whiteboard
- Treasure Hunt
- Tape Recording

CHRIST CENTERED

- Testimony
- Prayer
- Scriptures
- Service projects
- Building Faith
- Listen for the Spirit
- Temple Attendance
- Devotionals
- Church Standards
- Unconditional Love

MUSIC

Music can effectively teach and invite the Spirit almost better than any other teaching technique. Included with each lesson are suggestions for songs the class could sing or simply learn from by reading the lyrics. Inviting others in your ward to provide special musical numbers during your lessons binds hearts together and uplifts everyone. You can find the LDS hymnbook online at www.lds.org/music.

You can download songs, listen to them online, and do searches by topics, titles, and even scriptures! You can also use songs from Seminary, Young Women, Primary, and other music that has been published in Church magazines. Also on the Church's website are learning materials, such as how to conduct music, understand symbols and terms, and where to find great ideas to add variety to singing.

Check out these great resources:

- itunes.apple.com/us/app/lds-hymns/id332640791?mt=8 (Church Hymns on iTunes)
- freewardchoirmusic.com (Free LDS musical arrangements)
- www.soundsmithmusic.com (Free LDS music)

QUOTES

Quotes from Church authorities can be used to inspire the mind and uplift the heart. It's nice to have some quotes written on the board at the front of the room for students to read before class starts to set the tone and to get them thinking about the topic. Some of the suggested handouts in the book use such quotes, but you can also design your own handouts with your favorite quotes. Do a search at www.lds.org with a keyword about the topic you're searching for. More can be found online at:

- www.quotegarden.com
- www.thinkexist.com
- www.inspirational-quotes.info
- www.brainyquote.com
- www.quotationspage.com
- www.wisdomquotes.com

ARTWORK

Beautiful artwork can teach in a way that words alone cannot, especially for visual learners. Your church building's library may have some larger prints of older pictures. The pictures suggested in this book come from the newer Gospel Art Book (GAB).

You can purchase a "Gospel Art Book" (GAB) from Church Distribution at store.lds.org. It comes as a spiral-bound book containing 137 color pictures and a useful index that connects each image to the scriptures. It's an inexpensive and perfect investment for your own family's family home evening lessons! They are organized into the following six categories:

1. Old Testament
2. New Testament
3. Book of Mormon
4. Church History
5. Gospel in Action
6. Latter-day Prophets

You can access more pictures on the Church's website at www.lds.org/media-library/images. There you can find cool "memes" (inspirational picture quotes), desktop wallpapers, and the ever-popular Mormonads.

The pictures online are organized into almost every category you can imagine. The site also allows you to create images, as well as share your own photos and videos! Get in the habit of checking the Church's website often because there are always new features being added.

Here are some terrific Church resources that provide excellent artwork on gospel themes:

- www.lds.org/media-library/images (LDS images)
- relarchive.byu.edu (BYU religious education image archive)
- josephsmith.net (Joseph Smith Resource Center—maps, artwork, photos, documents, and more!)
- www.lds.org/scriptures/bible-photos (Photographs of scriptural sites)
- www.lds.org/scriptures/history-photos (Photographs of Church History sites)
- www.lds.org/temples/photo-gallery (Temple photos)

VIDEOS

The Church has some excellent videos that can be found and downloaded to your computer. You'll need a projector and either a white wall or screen in order to share them with your class.

A fantastic series of videos that is available online is called "The Life of Jesus Christ Bible videos." You can find them at www.lds.org/bible-videos, where new ones are being constantly added. You can also download a free mobile app for viewing.

YouTube hosts several "channels" of videos officially released by the Church as well at:

- www.youtube.com/user/MormonMessages
- www.youtube.com/user/LDSPublicAffairs

You'll find a lot of other great LDS videos on YouTube that were uploaded by members of the Church. Many chapels have Internet access, but be sure to do a test run with your equipment before you decide to include videos in your lesson. Your lessons shouldn't be entertainment focused, but spirit focused.

ARTICLES

What a blessing it is to read from Church leaders each month in the various Church magazines. Teach your class how to find material they can share with their families during family home evening lessons or to help them prepare sacrament talks in the future. Each lesson in this book includes only a few suggested articles, but there are so many more! One of the biggest blessings of preparing your lessons each month will be the focused time you get to spend researching specific gospel topics. You will learn so much more than you'll ever have time to share with your sisters or brothers in class on Sunday! Teaching Relief Society or Priesthood is a wonderful excuse to truly immerse yourself in gospel study. Enjoy it!

OBJECT LESSONS

Object lessons capture the students' interest and increase understanding by teaching the concept in a unique way. The Savior often used physical objects that were familiar to His listeners to illustrate simple principles. Each lesson offers ideas for object lessons that could be an effective introduction to the topic or a fun way to keep the class engaged.

CHALLENGES

A meaningful addition to each lesson is the use of a personal challenge that you can share with the class at the end of each lesson. Perhaps it should be called an "invitation for application." The class members need to APPLY what they've learned after they leave your classroom. If they don't USE the lesson material to improve their lives and strengthen their testimonies, then they aren't growing spiritually from your efforts. You can offer the suggested challenge, one of your own, or invite the class to choose their own personal goal that will allow them to delve deeper and stretch further. In the end, we won't be judged by all of the religious trivia we can recite to the Lord at the judgment seat, but by the Christlike qualities we have acquired. The Lord cares much more about what we are becoming than what we are doing.

SEMINARY DOCTRINAL MASTERY PASSAGES

Parents of seminary students may want to learn some of the same 100 scripture passages that their teens are learning to strengthen their home and family. They used to be called Scripture Mastery. Teachers can mention which verses correlate with each lesson's topic. What a terrific tool it is to commit scriptures to memory together. You can see all of the seminary manuals and resources at www.lds.org/si/seminary/manuals.

PREACH MY GOSPEL

The Church is currently experiencing a wonderful wave of missionaries as the Lord hastens His work. To help the sisters and brothers in your ward become more familiar with this missionary service guide, consider including topical passages and talk about how to share your lesson material with nonmember friends. You can see a free copy of the manual at www.lds.org/manual/preach-my-gospel-a-guide-to-missionary-service.

RESOURCES

Visit the Church's website section that is dedicated to Relief Society resources under the "Serve and Teach" menu tab on the home page at www.lds.org. When you click on "Resources," you will discover all kinds of fantastic tools to help you in your sacred calling! Click on "Leadership Training Library" to see even more helpful tools. There is so much to see.

The steps suggested for how to prepare a lesson include the following:

- Use approved lesson materials.
- Seek the guidance of the Spirit.
- Study your lesson in advance.
- Consider the needs of your ward and class members.
- Organize the lesson.
- Seek the gift of teaching.

Jesus was the master teacher. He still is! He cared deeply about each person He taught. He used variety, honesty, symbolism, and storytelling. He challenged His listeners to make specific changes in their lives. The more you study and teach the gospel, the greater will be your own understanding.

Use the scriptures each time you teach and encourage your class to feast from their pages. As you come to love the scriptures, your class will feel that passion and be inspired to feast upon them as well. Your task as a teacher is to invite your class to "come unto Christ." In order to do that effectively you must create an atmosphere where the Holy Ghost will be welcome and able to testify to the hearts of your students.

You give voice to the gospel principles taught each week, but it is the testifying power of the Holy Ghost that touches the hearts and transforms lives. May you feel the Spirit guide and direct you as you do your best to magnify this calling!

* *

ARTICLES ABOUT TEACHING WITH THE SPIRIT

Henry B. Eyring, "Rise To Your Call," *Ensign,* Nov. 2002.

William D. Oswald, "Gospel Teaching—Our Most Important Calling," *Ensign,* Nov. 2008.

Dallin H. Oaks, "Gospel Teaching," *Ensign,* Nov. 1999.

Bruce R. McConkie, "The Teacher's Divine Commission," *Ensign,* Apr. 1979.

David M. McConkie, "Gospel Learning and Teaching," *Ensign,* Nov. 2010.

"Teach by the Spirit": www.lds.org/manual/teaching-in-the-saviors-way /part-2-teach-by-the-spirit/teach-by-the-spirit

VIDEOS ABOUT TEACHING WITH THE SPIRIT

"Prepare and Teach by the Spirit": www.lds.org/media-library/video/2015 -12-3000-prepare-and-teach-by-the-spirit

'If We Teach by the Spirit": www.lds.org/media-library/video/2010-07-142 -if-we-teach-by-the-spirit

"Fundamentals of Gospel Teaching and Learning": www.lds.org/media -library/video/annual-mutual-theme/2-fundamentals-of-gospel-teaching -and-learning

"Teach Me to Walk in the Light": www.lds.org/media-library/video/2014 -01-1000-teach-me-to-walk-in-the-light

"Learning and Teaching in the Home and the Church": www.lds.org/media -library/video/2014-06-002-learning-and-teaching-in-the-home-and -the-church-the-church

First Sunday

Counseling Together about Local Needs

Councils

MUSIC

"Sweet Is the Work," *Hymns*, no. 147
"Awake, Ye Saints of God, Awake!" *Hymns*, no. 17
"We Meet, Dear Lord," *Hymns*, no. 151
"Truth Reflects upon Our Senses," *Hymns*, no. 273
"Love One Another," *Hymns*, no. 308

SUMMARY

Councils have been used since the premortal world! As we gather together, we learn how to better minister to one another and become more like Jesus Christ. We are reminded of the scripture that teaches us of the importance of His Spirit in our unified efforts, "Where two or three are gathered together in my name, as touching one thing, behold, there will I be in the midst of them—even so am I in the midst of you" (D&C 6:32).

That scripture teaches us the inspired formula for obtaining revelation and making decisions in the kingdom of God. The Church handbook explains that councils are an important part of keeping order and blessing families and individuals. The focus of all church councils is to help "individuals build testimonies, receive saving ordinances, keep covenants, and become consecrated followers of Jesus Christ" (*Handbook 2*, 4.4).

In the Church, we have a variety of different kinds of councils, including the Council of the First Presidency and Quorum of the Twelve Apostles, ward councils, stake disciplinary councils, and even family councils. All have the same goal of helping individuals come unto Christ. When everyone serving on the council has a voice and can feel unity and Christlike love, miracles can occur. An effective council uses the unique voice and talents of each person in order to make the best decisions.

While salvation is an individual, personal journey, it is also one that is designed to require the love and support of others. Heavenly Father sent us to earth together! His great Plan of Happiness includes learning how to live, serve, love, and work together as one.

· ·

QUOTES

- "The Lord's objective is that we become His—that we become one with Him, with our Heavenly Father, and with each other. The process is as important as the result. Councils are part of the divinely appointed process by which unity is achieved and by which we become Christ's." (Jakob R. Jones, "Gathered Together in My Name," *Ensign,* Sept. 2016.)
- "I have no hesitancy in giving you the assurance, if you will confer in council as you are expected to do, God will give you solutions to the problems that confront you." (President Stephen L. Richards, Conference Report, Oct. 1953, 86.)
- "They [councils] are called to preside and to lead and to extend God's love to His children." (M. Russell Ballard, "Counseling with Our Councils," *Ensign,* May 1994.)
- "Brothers and sisters, let us work together as never before in our stewardships to find ways to make more effective use of the wondrous power of councils." (M. Russell Ballard, "Counseling with Our Councils," *Ensign,* May 1994.)
- "The genius of our Church government is government through councils. Hardly a day passes but that I see . . . God's wisdom, in creating councils to govern His kingdom." (President Stephen L. Richards, Conference Report, Oct. 1953, 86.)
- "Ward council members strive to stay informed about the needs, well-being, and spiritual progress of members of their organizations. All of this happened because of the inspired work of a faithful ward council functioning according to the program that God has outlined for His children through His servants." (Elder M. Russell Ballard, "Blessed by Councils," *Ensign*, June 2011.)

· ·

GOSPEL ART

Adam and Eve Teaching Their Children (5 GAB)
Calling of the Fishermen (37 GAB)
Jesus Carrying a Lost Lamb (64 GAB)
King Benjamin Addresses His People (74 GAB)
Captain Moroni Raises the Title of Liberty (79 GAB)
The Foundation of the Relief Society (98 GAB)
Exodus from Nauvoo (411 KIT, 99 GAB)
Handcart Pioneers Approaching the Salt Lake Valley (102 GAB)
Service (115 GAB)

VIDEOS

"Working Together as One": www.lds.org/media-library/video/2013-06-036-working-together-as-one

"Share and Counsel Together": www.lds.org/media-library/video/2015-12-9000-share-and-counsel-together

"Ward Councils and Ward Mission Leaders": www.lds.org/training/wwlt/2013/hastening/ward-council-and-mission-leaders

"Helping Ward Councils": www.lds.org/media-library/video/2014-06-1400-helping-ward-councils

"Counseling with Our Councils": www.lds.org/general-conference/1994/04/counseling-with-our-councils

"Strength in Counsel": www.lds.org/general-conference/1993/10/strength-in-counsel

ARTICLES

Jakob R. Jones, "Gathered Together in My Name," *Ensign*, Sept. 2016.
M. Russell Ballard, "Blessed by Councils," *Ensign*, June 2011.
"Service in Councils Essential to 'Divine Organization' of Savior's Church": www.lds.org/church/news/service-in-councils-essential-to-divine-organization-of-saviors-church
M. Russell Ballard, "Family Councils: A Conversation with Elder and Sister Ballard," *Ensign*, June 2003.
Barbara B. Smith, "The Relief Society Role in Priesthood Councils," *Ensign*, Nov. 1979.

OBJECT LESSONS

-◆ Explain how teaching is more like playing soccer than playing tennis. The teacher should ask questions that inspire dialogue that bounces around the classroom, and not just back to the teacher. Sit in a circle or a U-shape during the lesson if possible. Using a ball, ask a question to someone in the class and toss him or her a ball. That person has to answer the question and then ask another question related to that same topic, tossing the ball to someone else in the room. Do that several times to get them used to the idea of a group dialogue. You could even continue to use the ball during the entire lesson to reinforce the idea of a unified lesson that involves everyone.

-◆ Give one person in the class a task to perform, such as carrying a dozen random objects. After attempting the task, ask the class members to suggest other ways to perform the same task. Let the person try one or two of the other methods and point out how "two heads are better than one!" Now, invite a few other people to work together to perform the task. Talk about how a council can benefit from several people's different perspectives and ideas, as well as combining the efforts into a successful plan of action.

-◆ To encourage the sisters or brothers to get to know each other better, choose some of the team building games on this fun web site: www.ventureteambuilding.co.uk/team-building-activities. Talk about how you will be counseling together each month in your Sunday lessons.

CHALLENGE

Create a list of all the benefits of counseling with others in making a decision. If you have a family, pick a date when you can hold a family council. The Church provides a helpful "Beginner's Guide to Family Councils" at www.lds.org/blog/the-beginners-guide-to-family-councils.

DOCTRINAL MASTERY PASSAGES

- Jacob 2:18–19
- Mosiah 2:17
- Abraham 3:22–23
- Joshua 24:15
- Daniel 2:44–45
- Matthew 16:15–19
- Ephesians 4:11–14
- D&C 18:10, 15–16
- D&C 84:33–39

· ·

PREACH MY GOSPEL

3, 8, 18, 19, 22, 31, 33, 66, 67, 68, 69, 71, 82, 88, 92, 93, 97, 115, 138, 144, 145, 146, 147, 148, 149, 156, 157, 168, 169, 170, 187, 197, 219

· ·

NOTES

_____

_____

_____

_____

_____

_____

_____

_____

_____

_____

_____

_____

_____

_____

_____

_____

_____

Missionary Work

MUSIC

"Called to Serve," *Hymns*, no. 249

"How Will They Know?" *Children's Songbook*, 182

"I Hope They Call Me on a Mission," *Children's Songbook*, 169

"I Want to Be a Missionary Now," *Children's Songbook*, 168

"We'll Bring the World His Truth (Army of Helaman)," *Children's Songbook*, 172

SUMMARY

Many people in the world are pure in heart and would embrace the fulness of the gospel if they were given the opportunity. We have been given the knowledge of saving ordinances, as well as the divinely commissioned authority to provide them to the nations of the earth.

When we truly feel the Savior's love, we have the natural desire to extend it to those around us. When we do, our joy will be felt for eternity. The Lord entrusts us with this important work, and it is our privilege to bring light to a dark world. Our righteous examples can illuminate our neighborhoods and draw the pure in heart to us.

When we help prepare young men and women to serve full-time missions and support them with prayers, food, finances, and referrals while they are laboring in the field, the Lord is pleased with our missionary efforts, and we will have an even greater desire to open our mouths and share what we know with a world that is seeking truth and direction. What a thrill it is to be a part of the exciting wave of missionary work happening right now as the Lord hastens His work!

In the spirit of love and kindness, our missionary work is about inviting people, not convincing them, to learn more. Rather than debate doctrine with non-believers, we gently love them and show them the Savior's love. The most important part of effective missionary work is not our carefully chosen words, but the Spirit with which we teach. This is the Lord's work and one of the most important things we can do here on earth.

As a council, talk about how your ward or branch could reach out to the community to build relationships with other churches, organizations, and individuals.

QUOTES

- "This isn't missionary work. This is missionary fun." (Neil L. Anderson, "It's a Miracle," *Ensign*, May 2013.)
- "We must develop love for people. Our hearts must go out to them in the pure love of the gospel, in a desire to lift them, to build them up, to point them to a higher, finer life that eventually will lead to exaltation in the celestial kingdom of God." (Ezra Taft Benson, "Keys to Successful Member-Missionary Work," *Ensign*, Sept. 1990.)
- "For the Savior's mandate to share the gospel to become part of who we are, we need to make member missionary work a way of life." (Quentin L. Cook, "Be a Missionary All Your Life," *Ensign*, Sept. 2008.)
- "It is impractical for us to expect that full-time missionaries alone can warn the millions in the world. Members must be finders. If we are in tune, the Spirit of the Lord will speak to us and guide us to those with whom we should share the gospel. The Lord will help us if we will but listen." (Spencer W. Kimball, "President Kimball's Vision of Missionary Work," *Ensign,* July 1985.)
- "When we received the special blessing of knowledge of the gospel of Jesus Christ and took upon ourselves the name of Christ by entering the waters of baptism, we also accepted the obligation to share the gospel with others." (L. Tom Perry, *Ensign*, Nov. 2009, 75.)
- "The standard of truth has been erected: no unhallowed hand can stop the work from progressing, persecution may rage, mobs may combine, armies may assemble, calumny may defame, but the truth of God will go forth boldly, nobly, and independent till it has penetrated every continent, visited every clime, swept every country, and sounded in every ear, till the purposes of God shall be accomplished and the great Jehovah shall say the work is done." (Joseph Smith, Church History, *Times & Seasons*, 1 March 1842, 709.)

➳ "After all that has been said, the greatest and most important duty is to preach the Gospel." (Joseph Smith, History of the Church, 2:478.)

GOSPEL ART

Daniel Refusing the King's Meat and Wine (23 GAB)
Esther (21 GAB)
Boy Jesus in the Temple (34 GAB)
Calling of the Fishermen (37 GAB)
Mary and Martha (45 GAB)
Go Ye Therefore (61 GAB)
Abinadi before King Noah (75 GAB)
Alma Baptizes in the Waters of Mormon (76 GAB)
Ammon Defends the Flocks of King Lamoni (78 GAB)
Missionaries: Elders (109 GAB)
Missionaries: Sisters (110 GAB)

VIDEOS

"Missionary Work": www.lds.org/manual/preach-my-gospel/asl/chapter3 /lesson5#missionary-work
"The Church to Fill the Earth": www.lds.org/media-library/video/2010 -07-059-the-church-to-fill-the-earth
"Developing the Faith to Find": www.lds.org/media-library/video/2007 -04-024-developing-the-faith-to-find
"Loving and Serving Others": www.lds.org/media-library/video/2007-08 -01-loving-and-serving-others
"Why Mormons Send Missionaries Around the World": www.lds.org /media-library/video/2010-05-1190-why-mormons-send-missionaries -around-the-world

ARTICLES

Earl C. Tingey, "Missionary Service," *Ensign,* May 1998, 39–41.
Thomas S. Monson, "That All May Hear," *Ensign*, May 1996.
M. Russell Ballard, "Creating a Gospel-Sharing Home," *Ensign,* May 2007.
Dallin H. Oaks, "Sharing the Gospel," *Ensign*, Nov. 2001.

Dallin H Oaks, "The Role of Members in Conversion," *Ensign*, March 2003, 52.

Ezra Taft Benson, "President Kimball's Vision of Missionary Work," *Ensign,* July 1985.

W. Christopher Waddell, "The Opportunity of a Lifetime," *Ensign*, Nov. 2011.

. . . .

OBJECT LESSONS

- The spirit of missionary work will fill your classroom as you invite the sisters or brothers to share their conversion stories.

- Invite the sisters or brothers to be creative in pairs and take turns doing "door approaches" by knocking on the door to your classroom and presenting a gospel message. You'll be amazed at how innovative they'll be!

- Set up a row of dominoes on the front table and then watch the chain reaction as you knock the first one down. Compare that to all of the lives that are touched for good by just one member of the Church being a good missionary.

- Display a large basket of goodies on the table at the front of the class and begin to eat from it, expressing great delight. Ask the class to share why they love the gospel so much. Continue snacking and then explain that when we enjoy the blessings of the gospel without sharing it with others, it's like you're having a basket of goodies that you love and not sharing it with the class! Pass the basket around and invite everyone to join you in eating yummy treats. At the end of the lesson, ask the sisters or brothers how many of them didn't take a treat, ate it right away, or planned on saving it for later. Explain that doing missionary work is similar—even when we share the sweet gospel with others, some people will accept and embrace it, others won't at all, and others might but not after many years.

- Invite the full-time missionaries to share some conversion stories and experiences with your class.

- Before class, put a bunch of pieces of candy in a bag. Tell the class that we often feel we can't make any difference as just one person. Show one piece of candy and explain that it represents you, a member of the Church. Show another piece of candy, which represents one person you talk to about the gospel. That person then tells someone else about the gospel, who tells another person and so on. Add a piece of candy next to each person who talks about the gospel. Talk about how our simple efforts can grow the Church exponentially. Pass around the candy to the class, illustrating that sharing the gospel can be SWEET!

CHALLENGE

Invite the full-time missionaries in your area over to dinner. Ask them about their investigators and find out what you can do to help. Invite them to teach one of their investigators in your home or go with them to teach.

DOCTRINAL MASTERY PASSAGES

- Moroni 10:4–5
- Isaiah 29:13–14
- Jeremiah 16:16
- Romans 1:16
- Revelation 14:6–7
- Joseph Smith History 1:15–20
- D&C 18:10, 15–16

PREACH MY GOSPEL

1, 2, 4–5, 8–13, 19, 20–21, 44–45, 81, 105, 107, 108, 127, 138, 139, 155–58, 174–76, 182-187, 190–92, 195–99, 203

NOTES

Religious Freedom

MUSIC

"Choose the Right," *Hymns*, no. 239
"Choose the Right Way," *Children's Songbook*, 160
"Know This, That Every Soul Is Free," *Hymns*, no. 240
"I Will Follow God's Plan," *Children's Songbook*, 164
"Dare to Do Right," *Children's Songbook*, 158

SUMMARY

The First Amendment in the US Constitution assures us the freedom and right to worship how we want. The purest form of freedom is being able to believe something that is very personal to you. Being able to practice the religion of our conscience and heart was so important to the Founding Fathers that it was included in the very first amendment of the Bill of Rights. Civil liberties and civil rights have long been debated in countries across the globe, and now religious freedom is on the hot seat.

Showing love and kindness to people of other faiths is crucial to our being truly Christlike. We should never be contentious in our discussions with people of other faiths, but always respectful. That includes people who have no professed faith. Kindness is powerful. We also need to get involved in the conversation that is currently taking place in the legal, political arenas in order to protect our rights. If we don't stand up for religious freedom, we could lose it.

QUOTES

↝ "The faithful use of our agency depends upon our having religious freedom." (Robert D. Hales, "Preserving Agency, Protecting Religious Freedom," *Ensign,* May 2015.)

- "My beloved brothers and sisters, don't walk! Run! Run to receive the blessings of agency by following the Holy Ghost and exercising the freedoms God has given us to do His will." (Robert D. Hales, "Preserving Agency, Protecting Religious Freedom," *Ensign,* May 2015.)
- "The Bible is replete with admonitions to remember the mighty acts of God as He has intervened in history for His people. We are witnesses of His mighty, intervening hand in the world even today." (David B. Haight, "Filling the Whole Earth," *Ensign,* Apr. 1990.)
- "In our increasingly unrighteous world, it is essential that values based on religious belief be part of the public discourse." (Quentin L. Cook, "Let There Be Light," *Ensign*, Oct. 2010.)
- "It is not our frowning battlements, our bristling sea coasts, our army and our navy. . . . Our reliance is in the love of liberty which God has planted in us." (Abraham Lincoln, Speech at Edwardsville, Illinois, 11 Sept. 1858, quoted in John Bartlett, *Familiar Quotations,* [Boston: Little, Brown and Co., 1968], 636.)

GOSPEL ART

Adam and Eve Teaching Their Children (5 GAB)
Building the Ark (7 GAB)
Daniel Refusing the King's Food and Wine (23 GAB)
Three Men in the Fiery Furnace (25 GAB)
Daniel in the Lions' Den (26 GAB)
John the Baptist Baptizing Jesus (35 GAB)
Calling of the Fishermen (37 GAB)
Jesus at the Door (65 GAB)
Lehi Prophesying to the People of Jerusalem (67 GAB)
King Benjamin Addresses His People (74 GAB)
Abinadi before King Noah (75 GAB)
Samuel the Lamanite on the Wall (81 GAB)
Captain Moroni Raises the Title of Liberty (79 GAB)
Exodus from Nauvoo (99 GAB)

VIDEOS

"What Is Religious Freedom": www.lds.org/media-library/video/2013-11
-1020-what-is-religious-freedom
"Preserving Religious Freedom": www.lds.org/media-library/video/2013-11
-1030-preserving-religious-freedom
"Religious Freedom": www.lds.org/media-library/video/topics/religious-freedom

. . . .

ARTICLES

Robert D. Hales, "Preserving Agency, Protecting Religious Freedom," *Ensign,*
May 2015.
David B. Haight, "Filling the Whole Earth," *Ensign,* May 1990.
Quentin L. Cook, "Let There Be Light," *Ensign,* Oct. 2010.
Howard W. Hunter, "The Golden Thread of Choice," *Ensign,* Oct. 1989.
Russell M. Nelson, "Combating Spiritual Drift—Our Global Pandemic,"
Ensign, Oct. 1993.
Dallin H. Oaks, "Loving Others and Living with Differences," *Ensign,* Oct.
2014.

. . . .

OBJECT LESSONS

- Find one of those toys where you have to put objects through different
  shapes. Ask some volunteers to put the objects in the circle. Of course,
  not all of the pieces will fit. Talk about how there are wonderful people all
  over the world who love God, but worship differently than we do. There
  are many ways to love God and we should encourage and support those
  who are trying their best to know God better and include Him in their
  lives.
- Divide the class into teams and challenge them to build a bridge with
  different materials. Award a treat to the team that builds the most creative and sturdy bridge. Emphasize how different the bridges are from
  each other, yet how effective they still are (if they all work). Talk about
  how important it is to build bridges with people of other faiths in our
  community.
- Show some pictures (classical art or from the Church) and invite three
  groups of volunteers in the class to reenact the picture. Talk about how
  they are similar or different. Now, talk about how different religions show

their devotion and commitment. For example, Jews wear a yarmulke on their head, Muslim women wear head scarves called hijabs, and so on. All religions interpret scriptures differently, yet their lives can be beautiful works of art.

CHALLENGE

Find out who your congressmen and senators are. Contact them to find out what current legislation involves religious freedom in your state. Find out what you can do to inform others and get involved in making a positive difference.

DOCTRINAL MASTERY PASSAGES

- 1 Nephi 3:7
- 2 Nephi 2:27
- 2 Nephi 28:7–9
- Jacob 2:18–19
- Mosiah 3:19
- Mosiah 4:30
- Alma 34:32–34
- Alma 41:10
- Helaman 5:12
- Moroni 7:16–17
- Moroni 7:45
- Exodus 20:3-17
- Joshua 1:8
- Isaiah 1:18
- Matthew 6:24
- John 7:17
- John 14:15
- 1 Corinthians 10:13
- Revelation 20:12–13
- D&C 1:37–38
- D&C 14:7
- D&C 58:26–27

PREACH MY GOSPEL

47–49, 66, 72, 75, 88, 150–51

NOTES

_____

_____

_____

_____

_____

Service & Charity

MUSIC

"A Poor Wayfaring Man of Grief," *Hymns*, no. 29
"As Sisters in Zion" (Women), *Hymns*, no. 309
"Because I Have Been Given Much," *Hymns*, no. 219
"Have I Done Any Good?" *Hymns*, no. 223
"Let Us Oft Speak Kind Words," *Hymns*, no. 232
"Love One Another," *Hymns*, no. 308

SUMMARY

How can you tell a true disciple of Jesus Christ? By the way he or she treats other people! One way we show the Lord how much we love Him is by serving His children, our brothers and sisters. When we feel God's love deep inside our soul, we feel a desire to reach outside ourselves and bless others. A true understanding of the gospel of Jesus Christ compels us to love and serve.

If we want to be like Christ, we need to do as Christ did: serve. The Savior ministered daily to the needs of those around Him. When we open our spiritual eyes, we will see many opportunities around us for Christlike service and love. Loving and serving our neighbor isn't always easy, but that great feeling you get afterwards is evidence that you're doing exactly what the Savior would do!

The gospel of Jesus Christ can be summed up in one word: love. The Spirit of the Lord is gentle and kind and influences us to do good and be good. We need to be patient with others as they learn and grown, and not look for their faults, just as we would hope they would do for us. When we show kindness inside and outside our home, hearts are softened and peace is given to a troubled world.

Charity is the pure love of Christ and the greatest of all virtues. Charity cannot be developed in the abstract; it requires clinical, hands-on experience. It is a process, not an event. The more we serve others the more genuine our love will become for others.

Introduce the members in your class to several great websites where they can go with their families to choose service projects in their area and reach out to others in their community:

- www.servenet.org
- www.idealist.org
- www.volunteers.org
- www.volunteermatch.org
- www.nationalservice.gov

. . . .

QUOTES

⊷ "Kindness is the essence of greatness and the fundamental characteristic of the noblest men and women I have known. Kindness is a passport that opens doors and fashions friends. It softens hearts and molds relationships that can last lifetimes." (Joseph B. Wirthlin, "The Virtue of Kindness," *Ensign,* May 2005.)

⊷ "Kindness has many synonyms—love, service, charity. But I like the word *kindness* because it implies action. It seems like something you and I can do. Kindness can be shown in so many ways." (Betty Jo Jepsen, "Kindness—A Part of God's Plan," *Ensign,* Nov. 1990.)

⊷ "We learn that charity, though often quantified as the action, is actually the state of the heart that prompts us to love one another." (Elaine Jack, "Strengthened in Charity," *Ensign,* Oct. 1996.)

⊷ "I am convinced that true brotherly love is essential to our happiness and to world peace. We need to show our love, beginning in the home and then widening our circle of love to encompass our ward members, our less active and nonmember neighbors, and also those who have passed beyond the veil." (Jack H. Goaslind, Jr., "Reach Out to Our Father's Children," *Ensign,* May 1981.)

⊷ "Charity is not just a precept or a principle, nor is it just a word to describe actions or attitudes. Rather, it is an internal condition that must be developed and experienced in order to be understood." (C. Max Caldwell, *Ensign,* Nov. 1992, 29–30.)

⊷ "When you get the Spirit of God, you feel full of kindness, charity, long-suffering, and you are willing all the day long to accord to every man that which you want yourself." (John Taylor, *Teachings of the Presidents of the Church: John Taylor.*)

↝ "The more we serve our fellowmen in appropriate ways, the more substance there is to our souls." (Spencer W. Kimball, *New Era*, Mar. 1981, 47–49.)

. . . .

GOSPEL ART

Jesus Christ (1 GAB)
City of Zion Is Taken Up (6 GAB)
The Sermon on the Mount (39 GAB)
Christ Healing the Sick at Bethesda (42 GAB)
The Good Samaritan (44 GAB)
Jesus Washing the Apostles' Feet (55 GAB)
Jesus Carrying a Lost Lamb (64 GAB)
King Benjamin Addresses His People (74 GAB)
Jesus Healing the Nephites (83 GAB)
Jesus Blesses the Nephite Children (84 GAB)
The Foundation of the Relief Society (98 GAB)
Service (115 GAB)
Young Couple Going to the Temple (120 GAB)

. . . .

VIDEOS

"Love One Another": www.lds.org/media-library/video/2010-02-04-love-one
-another
"Lessons I Learned as a Boy": www.lds.org/media-library/video/2009-01
-01-gordon-hinckley-lessons-i-learned-as-a-boy
"Love Thy Neighbor": www.youtube.com/watch?v=lq5IzDW4ufA
"Charity: An Example of the Believers": www.youtube.com/watch?v=A
-ih_ZkaKC0&feature=youtube_gdata
"We Believe in Doing Good to All Men: Service": www.youtube.com/watch
?v=VXdTNEri1GE&feature=youtube_gdata
"The Good Samaritan": www.lds.org/media-library/video/1998-05-01-the
-good-samaritan?category=feature-films
"David Andre Koch, Feed My Sheep": www.lds.org/media-library/video
/2012-03-06-david-andre-koch-feed-my-sheep
"Feed My Lambs": www.lds.org/media-library/video/2012-06-1880-feed-my
-lambs

"Being a More Christian Christian": www.lds.org/media-library/video/2012
-10-5010-elder-robert-d-hales
"Ye Have Done It Unto Me": www.lds.org/media-library/video/2011-10-068
-ye-have-done-it-unto-me

* *

ARTICLES

Joseph B. Wirthlin, "The Virtue of Kindness," *Ensign*, May 2005.
Betty Jo Jepsen, "Kindness—A Part of God's Plan," *Ensign,* Nov. 1990.
Milly Day, "Kindness, Goodwill, Generosity," *Ensign*, Jan. 1998.
Susan Hainsworth, "If You Would Serve Them, Love Them," *Ensign,* Mar.
    1986.
C. Max Caldwell, "Love of Christ," Nov. 1992, 29–30.
Elaine L. Jack, "Strengthened in Charity," Nov. 1996, 91–93.
Gene R. Cook, "Charity: Perfect and Everlasting Love," May 2002, 82–83.
Bonnie D. Parkin, "Choosing Charity: That Good Part," Nov. 2003, 104–106.
Henry B. Eyring, "Feeding His Lambs," *Ensign*, Feb. 2008.
Derek A. Cuthbert, "The Spirituality of Service," May 1990, 12–13.
Jeffrey R. Holland, "Charity Never Faileth," *Ensign*, March 2011.
V. Dallas Merrell, "A Vision of Service," *Ensign*, Dec. 1996, 10–15.
Spencer W. Kimball, "Small Acts of Service," *Ensign*, Dec. 1974, 2–7.
Russell C. Taylor, "The Joy of Service," *Ensign*, Nov. 1984, 23–24.
Gene R. Cook, "Charity: Perfect and Everlasting Love," *Ensign*, May 2002,
    82–83.

* *

OBJECT LESSONS

↪ Make "Friendship Fudge" during the lesson by passing around gallon size
bags of ingredients that the members have to squish together to form the
sweet treat. Recipe:

- 4 cups powdered sugar
- 3 oz. softened cream cheese
- 1/2 cup softened margarine
- 1/2 cup cocoa
- 1 tsp. vanilla
- 1/2 cup chopped nuts

    When it is mixed together, roll it into a log and slice and serve.

↪ Have a contest with prizes to see which of the class members have the
longest hair, largest key ring, highest shoe heels, heaviest church bag, etc.
You can bring a scale and ruler to determine winners. Next, ask who has

the most Christlike love? Talk about how we can measure that quality. Can it be measured? Someone once said, "How can you tell a true disciple of Christ? By the way she treats other people."

↪ Teach the class members how to knit or crochet so that during your lesson they can begin making leper bandages to send to the Church's Humanitarian Center! You'll find tons of things your Relief Society can do to serve at www.ldsphilanthropies.org Items can be sent to:

> LDS Philanthropies
> 15 E. South Temple
> 2nd Floor East
> Salt Lake City, UT 84150
> Telephone: (801) 240-5567

↪ While teaching your lesson, remove your jacket, belt, and shoes. Unbutton some buttons on your sleeves, without explaining why. (Be modest!) At the end, say "You probably won't remember a word I said by the time you get home, but you will never forget what I did. Actions speak louder than words." We can talk about being Christlike, but when we serve we truly are Christlike.

↪ Pass around a mirror and ask the members to look in it. Ask them when they focused on their own image if they were able to see anyone else? (No.) By serving others we focus less on our own problems and challenges and gain improved perspective.

• •

CHALLENGE

Talk to your Relief Society president or compassionate service leader to see what you can do to serve. Who needs help in your ward? Your service can be anonymous or even performed by your entire family.

• •

DOCTRINAL MASTERY PASSAGES

- 2 Nephi 28:7–9
- 3 Nephi 11:29
- Leviticus 19:18
- Jacob 2:18–19
- Moroni 7:45
- D&C 64:9–11
- Mosiah 2:17
- Moses 7:18
- D&C 88:123–24

• •

PREACH MY GOSPEL

2, 8, 62, 87, 115, 118, 123–26, 168–69

• •

NOTES

Trials & Opposition

MUSIC

"Choose the Right," *Hymns*, no. 239
"I Will Follow God's Plan," *Children's Songbook*, 164
"Arise, O Glorious Zion," *Hymns*, no. 40
"Cast Thy Burden upon the Lord," *Hymns*, no. 110
"Come, All Ye Saints of Zion," *Hymns*, no. 38
"Glorious Things Are Sung of Zion," *Hymns*, no. 48
"How Firm a Foundation," *Hymns*, no. 85
"I Need My Heavenly Father," *Children's Songbook*, 18

SUMMARY

By following Jesus Christ, we are choosing eternal life and liberty. If we follow Satan, we are selecting evil and eternal captivity. One of the purposes of mortality is to show which choices we'll make, so there must be opposition in all things in order for us to exercise agency.

The trials and tribulations we face will help us grow spiritually, refine us, and build our Christlike character. Adversity is designed to be a part of our earthly life experience to strengthen our physical and spiritual muscles. So, rather than question "Why me?" we should ask, "What can I learn from this experience?"

Our trials are designed to soften our hearts and bring us closer to Christ. We need not fear nor lose hope. Following the Savior will ease our burdens and lighten our loads. He has overcome the world and wants to help us do the same.

QUOTES

- "Repeated assurances have been given regarding the benefits and blessings of positive responses to adversity, however undeserved. The witness of the Spirit and the manifestation of greater things often follow the trial of one's faith. Spiritual refinement may be realized in the furnace of affliction. Thereby we may be prepared to experience personal and direct contact with God." (Ronald E. Poelman, "Adversity and the Divine Purpose of Mortality," *Ensign*, May. 1989.)

- "While the freedom to choose involves the risk of mistakes, it also offers the opportunity, through our Father's plan, to overcome them." (Spencer J. Condie, "Agency: The Gift of Choices," *Ensign,* Sept. 1995, 16–22.)

- "Rather than simply passing through trials, we must allow trials to pass through us in ways that sanctify us." (Neal A. Maxwell, "Enduring Well," *Ensign*, April 1997.)

- "We cannot expect to learn endurance in our later years if we have developed the habit of quitting when things get difficult now." (Robert D. Hales, " 'Behold, We Count Them Happy Which Endure,' " *Ensign*, May 1998.)

- "Paul, in describing our 'perilous times,' did not promise that things would necessarily get easier or necessarily better. He did give counsel to those seeking comfort and assurance in the face of the deteriorating conditions of our day. Just as his prophecies or predictions were clearly accurate, so is his direction to us remarkably relevant as well. Said he, 'Continue in the things which thou hast learned and hast been assured of, knowing of whom thou hast learned them.' " (Cecil O. Samuelson Jr, "Perilous Times," *Ensign,* Nov. 2004.)

GOSPEL ART

Ruth Gleaning in the Fields (17 GAB)
Building the Ark (7 GAB)
The Good Samaritan (44 GAB)
Parable of the Ten Virgins (53 GAB)
Jesus at the Door (65 GAB)
Lehi's Dream (69 GAB)
Enos Praying (72 GAB)
Captain Moroni Raises the Title of Liberty (79 GAB)
Two Thousand Young Warriors (80 GAB)

Emma Crossing the Ice (96 GAB)
The Foundation of the Relief Society (98 GAB)
Handcart Pioneers Approaching the Salt Lake Valley (102 GAB)
Service (115 GAB)
Noah and the Ark with Animals (8 GAB)
Three Men in the Fiery Furnace (25 GAB)
Daniel in the Lions' Den (26 GAB)
Abinadi before King Noah (75 GAB)
Samuel the Lamanite on the Wall (81 GAB)
Joseph Smith in Liberty Jail (97 GAB)

VIDEOS

"Be Not Troubled": www.lds.org/media-library/video/2010-07-038-be-not
-troubled
"Adversity": www.lds.org/media-library/video/topics/adversity
"Enduring It Well," Shauna Ewing: mormonchannel.org/enduring-it-well
/61-shauna-ewing-compassion-upon-you-part-2
"Come What May & Love It": www.lds.org/media-library/video/2009-01
-03-come-what-may-and-love-it

ARTICLES

Richard G. Scott, "The Sustaining Power of Faith in Times of Uncertainty
and Testing," *Ensign,* May 2003.
Cecil O. Samuelson Jr., "Perilous Times," *Ensign*, Nov. 2004.
Boyd K. Packer, "The Test," *Ensign*, Nov. 2008.
Neal A. Maxwell, "Enduring Well," *Ensign,* April 1997.

OBJECT LESSONS

➼ Set up a game of Jenga or Stack Attack, or simply stack up wooden blocks
in a weave pattern. Invite class members to remove one of the blocks and
mention a trial in our lives, as well as a strength we gain when we suc-
cessfully triumph over the challenge. Eventually, the tower will fall and so
will our spirituality when we lose hope or stop following the Savior. We

don't always have the power to select our trials, but we always have the freedom to choose how we will respond to them.

➤ Show the class a piece of sandpaper and explain that it is carefully designed to not be too rough, but just rough enough to make a piece of wood smoother. This is similar to how the Lord allows us to be tested or tried in our lives, but not beyond what we can bear. He does this to make us stronger and more refined. (1 Corinthians 10:13; James 1:2–4).

➤ Have the class stand up and ask them to jump as high as they can, but with the stipulation that they can't bend their knees. (They won't be able to jump very high.) Now, instruct them to jump again, but this time they can bend their knees as low as they want to before launching upwards. Point out to them that the only way to jump high is to bend low first. When we are brought low with trials or difficulties, we must remember that it takes that bending low to propel us higher. If we are brought low with trials, then we can build sufficient faith and trust in God so He can lift us to a higher spiritual place.

CHALLENGE

Each day is filled with challenges and problems to overcome. Sometimes we create our own problems by making bad choices, but often we are placed in difficult circumstances because of other reasons not of our own doing. Write a list of the trials in your life and the Christlike qualities you can develop as you endure and overcome them.

DOCTRINAL MASTERY PASSAGES

- 1 Nephi 3:7
- 2 Nephi 2:27
- 2 Nephi 28:7–9
- Jacob 2:18–19
- Mosiah 3:19
- Mosiah 4:30
- Alma 34:32–34
- Alma 41:10

- Helaman 5:12
- Moroni 7:16–17
- Moroni 7:45
- Exodus 20:3–17
- Joshua 1:8
- Isaiah 1:18
- Matthew 6:24
- John 7:17

- John 14:15
- 1 Corinthians 10:13
- Revelation 20:12–13
- D&C 1:37–38
- D&C 14:7
- D&C 58:26–27

PREACH MY GOSPEL

47–49, 66, 72, 75, 88, 150–51

. . . .

NOTES

Second & Third Sundays

General Conference Messages

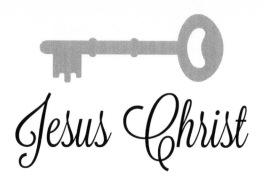

Jesus Christ

MUSIC

"I Know That My Redeemer Lives," *Hymns*, no. 136
"Jesus, Lover of My Soul," *Hymns*, no. 102
"I'm Trying to Be Like Jesus," *Children's Songbook*, 78
"The Lord Is My Light," *Hymns*, no. 89
"Jesus, the Very Thought of Thee," *Hymns*, no. 141
"Come Unto Jesus," *Hymns*, no. 117

SUMMARY

Jesus Christ is the Only Begotten Son of God and the Savior of the world. He was chosen and foreordained to come to Earth to atone for our sins and teach us how to return to our Heavenly Father. Our faith and hope are built upon the Savior's atoning sacrifice.

The most important event in the history of mankind was when the Savior was crucified for the world. Jesus Christ's Atonement took place in the Garden of Gethsemane and on the cross at Calvary. His redeeming sacrifice was necessary to ransom all people from the physical and spiritual effects of sin. Because of His merciful gift, everyone has the opportunity to repent, be forgiven of their sins, and be resurrected.

To thank Him for paying our spiritual and physical debts, we must show faith in Him, repent, be baptized, and follow Him. By following Jesus Christ, we can receive peace in this life and eternal joy in the life to come. We can build a testimony of Him through scripture study, prayer, and following His example.

QUOTES

- "The stories of Jesus can be like a rushing wind across the embers of faith in the hearts of our children. Jesus said, 'I am the way, the truth, and the life.' The stories of Jesus shared over and over bring faith in the Lord Jesus Christ and strength to the foundation of testimony. Can you think of a more valuable gift for our children?" (Neil L. Andersen, "Tell Me the Stories of Jesus," *Ensign*, May 2010.)
- "Each of us has the responsibility to know the Lord, love Him, follow Him, serve Him, teach and testify of Him." (Russell M. Nelson, "Jesus the Christ: Our Master and More," *Ensign,* Apr. 2000, 4–17.)
- "The soul that comes unto Christ dwells within a personal fortress, a veritable palace of perfect peace." (Jeffrey R. Holland, "Come unto Me," *Ensign,* Apr. 1998, 16–23.)
- "To follow Christ is to become like Him. It is to learn from His character. As spirit children of our Heavenly Father, we do have the potential to incorporate Christlike attributes into our life and character." (Dieter F. Uchtdorf, *"Developing Christlike Attributes,"* Ensign, Oct. 2008.)

GOSPEL ART

Isaiah Writes of Christ's Birth (22 GAB)
The Nativity (30 GAB)
Boy Jesus in the Temple (34 GAB)
John the Baptist Baptizing Jesus (35 GAB)
Calling of the Fishermen (37 GAB)
Christ Ordaining the Apostles (38 GAB)
Sermon on the Mount (39 GAB)
Jesus Blessing Jairus's Daughter (41 GAB)
Mary and Martha (45 GAB)
Triumphal Entry (50 GAB)
Jesus Washing the Apostles' Feet (55 GAB)
Jesus Praying in Gethsemane (56 GAB)
The Crucifixion (57 GAB)
Burial of Jesus (58 GAB)
Mary and the Resurrected Lord (59 GAB)
Jesus Shows His Wounds (60 GAB)
Go Ye Therefore (61 GAB)
The Ascension of Jesus (62 GAB)

Jesus at the Door (65 GAB)
The Second Coming (66 GAB)
The Resurrected Jesus Christ (66 GAB)
Christ Walking on the Water (43 GAB)
Christ and the Rich Young Ruler (48 GAB)
Jesus Christ Appears to the Nephites (82 GAB)
Jesus Blesses the Nephite Children (84 GAB)

VIDEOS

There are MANY videos to choose from in the Church's new Bible Videos about the Life of Jesus Christ found at www.lds.org/bible-videos.
"Jesus Declares He Is the Messiah": www.lds.org/media-library/video/2011-10-029-jesus-declares-he-is-the-messiah
"Are We Christians?": www.lds.org/pages/mormon-messages
See some of the great testimonies of Christ on www.mormonchannel.org/watch/series/bible-videos.

ARTICLES

Ezra Taft Benson, "Five Marks of the Divinity of Jesus Christ," *Ensign*, Dec. 2001.
Ezra Taft Benson, "Jesus Christ: Our Savior and Redeemer," *Ensign*, June 1990.
Russell M. Nelson, "Jesus the Christ: Our Master and More," *Ensign*, Apr. 2000.
Orson F. Whitney, "The Divinity of Jesus Christ," *Ensign*, Dec. 2003.

OBJECT LESSONS

☞ Show various objects and ask how they relate to Jesus Christ:
  » **Porch light:** serves as a beacon to help us find our way home
  » **Campfire:** provides warmth and comfort
  » **Lighthouse:** Offers light in the darkness, offers perspective in the storm
  » **Night-light:** banishes darkness and eliminates fear
  » **Car headlights:** lets us know where we are heading

> » **Lights in a movie theater:** a guide that can be followed
> » **Light bulb:** inspires us and brings us new light and understanding

➳ Pass around a beautiful rose, but with the thorns still intact. Talk about how fragrant and pleasing it is. Next, bruise some of the rose petals and point out the thorns. Jesus's body was bruised for our iniquities and a crown of thorns was placed on his head. Now ask someone to be a time-keeper and someone else to take the rose petals off the stem as fast as possible. Ask for another volunteer and timekeeper. Say "Okay, let's see if you can beat that time. Ready? Let's see you put it back together!" No matter how hard we try, we can't rebuild a rose, but God cannot only do that, but he can also restore life through Jesus Christ. We are even more beautiful than a rose and will all be resurrected because with God, all things are possible!

➳ Ask for a volunteer to stand in a square that is marked on the floor with masking tape. Show the volunteer a candy bar on the table and tell her she can have it only if she can reach it without leaving the square. Ask for another volunteer to help her. That's what the Savior did for us; He bridges the gap between mortality and eternal life. His Atonement gave us the gift of repentance so we taste the sweet love of Heavenly Father!

➳ Ask someone in the class to put on a sock. Hand the volunteer a muddy sock. The volunteer will probably not want to touch the dirty sock, so ask her what could be done to make her willing. Tell her you'll take the muddy sock and give her a clean, new one. The Savior took upon Him-self all of our dirty sins and gave us each a clean sock to wear when we return to our Father in Heaven, so that we will be clean from the sins of the world.

➳ Set out pictures of the Savior around the room. Invite class members to select one and talk about it. Without realizing it at first, the class's com-ments will turn into a very sweet testimony meeting of the Savior.

CHALLENGE

Write your testimony of Jesus Christ in your journal and share it with your family. Write it in a Book of Mormon and share it with a non-member.

DOCTRINAL MASTERY PASSAGES

- Helaman 5:12
- 3 Nephi 27:27

- Genesis 1:26–27
- Job 19:25–26
- Isaiah 53:3–5
- Matthew 16:15–19
- Luke 24:36–39
- John 3:5

- John 17:3
- Acts 7:55–56
- D&C 19:16–19
- D&C 76:22–24
- D&C 130:22–23
- 1 Corinthians 15:20–22

PREACH MY GOSPEL

34, 37, 47–48, 51–52, 60–61, 90, 105, 116, 123–126

NOTES

Faith

MUSIC

"Go Forth with Faith," *Hymns*, no. 263
"Come unto Him," *Hymns*, no. 114
"Faith of Our Fathers," *Hymns*, no. 84
"Testimony," *Hymns*, no. 137
"When Faith Endures," *Hymns*, no. 128
"True to the Faith," *Hymns*, no. 254

SUMMARY

The first principle of the gospel is faith in the Lord Jesus Christ. Faith is believing in Him with our spiritual eyes when we haven't seen Him with our physical eyes. It is a principle of action that compels us to pray, be obedient, and trust in His promises. We increase our faith by testing and studying His words. Faith has power to move mountains, perform miracles, and prove us worthy to see God.

Our faith can provide the light we need to live in a dark world. When doubts begin to enter our mind and heart, we need to hold on to the things we know to be true and the Lord will help us to build on that foundation.

QUOTES

- "Spiritual light rarely comes to those who merely sit in darkness waiting for someone to flip a switch. It takes an act of faith to open our eyes to the Light of Christ. Spiritual light cannot be discerned by carnal eyes." (Dieter F. Uchtdorf, "The Hope of God's Light," *Ensign*, May 2013.)

- "Faith is not only a feeling; it is a decision." (Neil L. Andersen, "You Know Enough," *Ensign*, Nov. 2008.)
- "Only faith in the Lord Jesus Christ and His Atonement can bring us peace, hope, and understanding." (Robert D. Hales, "Finding Faith in the Lord Jesus Christ," *Ensign,* Nov. 2004.)
- "We promote the process of strengthening our faith when we do what is right—increased faith always follows." (L. Whitney Clayton, "Help Thou Mine Unbelief," *Ensign,* Nov. 2001.)
- "Faith in Jesus Christ takes us beyond mere acceptance of the Savior's identity and existence. It includes having complete confidence in His infinite and eternal redemptive power." (James O. Mason, "Faith in Jesus Christ," *Ensign,* Apr. 2001.)
- "Faith in the Lord Jesus Christ is a conviction and trust that God knows us and loves us and will hear our prayers and answer them with what is best for us." (Dallin H. Oaks, "Faith in the Lord Jesus Christ," *Ensign,* May 1994.)

GOSPEL ART

Esther (21 GAB)
Jesus Calms the Storm (40 GAB)
Jesus Shows His Wounds (60 GAB)
Christ Walking on the Water (43 GAB)
Enos Praying (72 GAB)
Abinadi before King Noah (75 GAB)
Alma Baptizes in the Waters of Mormon (76 GAB)
Two Thousand Young Warriors (80 GAB)
Joseph Smith Seeks Wisdom in the Bible (89 GAB)
The First Vision (90 GAB)
Young Man Being Baptized (103 GAB)
Girl Being Baptized (104 GAB)

VIDEOS

"By Faith": www.lds.org/media-library/video/2016-03-018-by-faith
"Our Faith": www.lds.org/media-library/video/missionary/our-faith
"Faith": www.lds.org/media-library/video/topics/faith

"Light Switch": www.lds.org/media-library/video/2015-06-023-light-switch
?category=topics/faith

"Faith and Works": www.lds.org/media-library/video/2012-06-2060-faith
-and-works?category=topics/faith

"Faith and Trials": www.lds.org/media-library/video/2011-03-086-faith-and
-trials?category=topics/faith

"A Test of Faith": www.lds.org/media-library/video/2012-06-1240-a-test-of
-faith?category=topics/faith

ARTICLES

Neil L. Andersen, "Faith Is Not by Chance, but by Choice," *Ensign,* Oct,
2015.

Richard G. Scott, "Make the Exercise of Faith Your First Priority," *Ensign,*
Oct. 2014.

Russell M. Nelson, "Face the Future with Faith," *Ensign,* Apr. 2011.

Russell M. Nelson, "Let Your Faith Show," *Ensign,* Apr. 2014.

James E. Faust, "The Shield of Faith," *Ensign,* Apr. 2000.

Gordon B. Hinckley, "Faith: The Essence of True Religion," *Ensign*, Oct.
1995.

Russell M. Nelson, "Faith in Jesus Christ," *Ensign*, Mar. 2008.

Kevin W. Pearson, "Faith in the Lord Jesus Christ," *Ensign*, May 2009.

Gordon B. Hinckley, "The Cornerstones of Our Faith," *Ensign*, Nov. 1984.

Robert D. Hales, "Finding Faith in the Lord Jesus Christ," *Ensign*, Nov. 2004.

Gordon B. Hinckley, "Be Not Faithless," *Ensign*, Apr. 1989.

Quentin L. Cook, "Live By Faith and Not by Fear," *Ensign*, Nov. 2007.

OBJECT LESSONS

➤ Invite the class to sing "I Am a Child of God" and then tell them the story
behind the words. Originally the words read "Teach me all that I must
know to live with Him someday," but President Spencer W. Kimball said
that that's not enough—we have to DO. A leader doesn't just tell other
people what to do, but is willing to do them herself or himself as well.
Show people—don't just tell people.

➤ Ask for a brave volunteer who is willing to be blindfolded and show trust
in you. Spin her around a few times and tell her walk to the door. Give
her instructions every once in a while so it looks like she might run into

something, but when she gets close, have her turn and avoid running into anything. (The class will be worried for her.) Finally, tell her to sit down somewhere she wouldn't expect to be a chair. As she is walking towards the door, have someone place a chair in that spot. Have her take off the blindfold after she sits down and talk about what thoughts went through her mind. Talk about her doubts and the doubts of the class members who watched, as well as why it is so important to put trust in someone who will never deceive us (the Lord).

↦ Put clear vinegar in a clear glass so the class thinks it is filled with water. Ask the class what you could do to make the water overflow. Ask them to think very hard. Did that make any change? (No.) Add some baking soda and the vinegar will immediately begin to bubble up! In other words, we need to take action. When we act, our faith has more power!

• •

CHALLENGE

Write a list of all the gospel principles you KNOW to be true and HOW you came to that knowledge and understanding. This will be the beginning of a wonderful testimony journal!

• •

DOCTRINAL MASTERY PASSAGES

- 1 Nephi 3:7
- Mosiah 4:30
- Alma 32:21
- Ether 12:6
- Ether 12:27
- Moroni 7:45

- Moroni 10:4–5
- Proverbs 3:5–6
- Matthew 5:14–16
- Romans 1:16
- 1 Corinthians 10:13
- Ephesians 4:11–14

- James 2:17–18
- Joseph Smith History 1:15–20
- D&C 1:37–38
- D&C 84:33–39

• •

PREACH MY GOSPEL

18, 22, 38, 61, 90–102, 115, 116, 155

• •

NOTES

_____

_____

_____

_____

_____

_____

_____

_____

_____

_____

_____

_____

_____

_____

_____

_____

_____

_____

_____

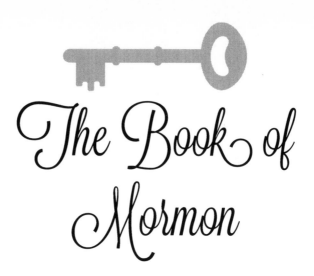

The Book of Mormon

MUSIC

"As I Search the Holy Scriptures," *Hymns*, no. 277
"Book of Mormon Stories," *Children's Songbook*, 118
"From Homes of Saints Glad Songs Arise," *Hymns*, no. 297
"The Books in the Book of Mormon," *Children's Songbook*, 119
"Search, Ponder, and Pray," *Children's Songbook*, 109

SUMMARY

We can find more comfort and wisdom in the Book of Mormon than in all other books ever caused to be written. The Book of Mormon is a sacred record that contains the fulness of the gospel and testifies that Jesus Christ is the Redeemer of the world.

The Law of Witnesses was fulfilled by three men who gave testimony when they saw an angel and the gold plates while hearing God's voice, as well as eight other men who handled the plates with their own hands. Each setting was different, but both experiences never left doubt in the minds and hearts of the witnesses for the rest of their lives. Each of us can be a witness of the Book of Mormon too.

QUOTES

- "Each of us, at some time in our lives, must discover the Book of Mormon for ourselves—and not just discover it once, but rediscover it again and again." (Spencer W. Kimball, "How Rare a Possession—the Scriptures!" *Ensign,* Sept. 1976, 2–5.)
- "I told the brethren that the Book of Mormon was the most correct of any book on earth, and the keystone of our religion, and a man would get nearer to God by abiding by its precepts than by any other book." (Joseph Smith Jr, *History of the Church of Jesus Christ of Latter-day Saints,* 4:461.)
- "I knew it was true, as well as I knew that I could see with my eyes, or feel by the touch of my fingers, or be sensible of the demonstration of any sense." (Brigham Young, *Journal of Discourses,* 3:91.)
- "The Book of Mormon is truly a witness for Jesus Christ and his plan of salvation for mankind. It is a witness that Jesus Christ, through Joseph Smith, has again established his work in our day. We invite all mankind to read it and learn for themselves its powerful message." (James A. Cullimore, "The Book of Mormon," *Ensign,* May 1976.)

GOSPEL ART

Mormon Abridging the Plates (306 KIT)
Moroni Hides the Plates in the Hill Cumorah (320 KIT, 86 GAB)
Christ Asks for the Records (323 KIT)
The Gold Plates (325 KIT)
The Bible and Book of Mormon: Two Witnesses (326 KIT)
Joseph Smith Seeks Wisdom in the Bible (402 KIT, 89 GAB)
Saving the Book of Commandments (409 KIT)
Translating the Book of Mormon (416 KIT)
Search the Scriptures (617 KIT)

VIDEOS

"A Book with a Promise": www.mormonchannel.org/watch/series/mormon
-messages/a-book-with-a-promise-2
"Prepared for Our Day": www.lds.org/media-library/video/2012-08-3110
-prepared-for-our-day

"Book of Mormon Testimonies": www.lds.org/media-library/video/2011
-06-8-book-of-mormon-testimonies

"Another Testament of Jesus Christ—Richard": lds.org/media-library/video
/truth-restored

"What is the role of the Book of Mormon": www.lds.org/manual/preach
-my-gospel/asl/chapter5

- -

ARTICLES

- Ezra Taft Benson, "The Book of Mormon is the Word of God," *Ensign*, Jan. 1988.
- Ezra Taft Benson, "The Book of Mormon and the Doctrine and Covenants," *Ensign*, May 1987.
- Daniel C. Peterson, "Mounting Evidence for the Book of Mormon," *Ensign,* Jan. 2000.
- L. Tom Perry, "Give Heed Unto the Word of the Lord," *Ensign*, June 2000.

- -

OBJECT LESSONS

- Show the class an old, rotten banana and ask for a volunteer to eat it. (No one will want to.) Ask the class why they don't think it will taste very good. Now hold up a good banana and ask why anyone would choose to eat this one. Explain that our lives are like fruit; people can tell what kind of people we are by the fruit we produce. Matthew 7:20 says, "Wherefore by their fruits ye shall know them." Ask, "What kind of fruit do you want to produce? The Book of Mormon is the fruit that evidences the truthfulness of Joseph Smith's testimony. You may be the only Book of Mormon people will ever 'read.' Live your lives so that others can tell you're a disciple of Christ and want to know more."
- Invite the class to write their testimonies of the Book of Mormon inside copies that the missionaries can give away to their investigators. Take a picture of the class members to include with their written testimony.
- Have the class draw pictures and quotes of the truthfulness of the Book of Mormon that could be turned into "memes" and uploaded to Pinterest on their boards. They could create memes that spotlight how the Book of Mormon has blessed their lives.

- -

CHALLENGE

Set a goal to read the Book of Mormon this year in your personal scripture study. Calculate how many pages a day you'll need to read to accomplish your objective.

DOCTRINAL MASTERY PASSAGES

- Alma 37:6–7
- Moroni 10:4–5
- Isaiah 29:13–14
- Ezekiel 37:15–17
- John 10:16

- 2 Thessalonians 2:1–3
- 2 Timothy 3:16–17
- James 1:5–6
- Revelation 14:6–7

PREACH MY GOSPEL

7, 38–39, 103-4, 110–11, 103–114, 130

NOTES

The Power of the Holy Ghost

MUSIC

"The Holy Ghost," *Children's Songbook*, 105
"The Still Small Voice," *Children's Songbook*, 106
"Dearest Children, God Is Near You," *Hymns*, no. 96
"God of Power, God of Right," *Hymns*, no. 20
"Great Is the Lord," *Hymns*, no. 77
"The Spirit of God," *Hymns*, no. 2

SUMMARY

The Holy Ghost has been sent to us by a loving Heavenly Father to provide comfort, guidance, and a witness for truth. The Holy Ghost is a member of the Godhead and has a distinct mission to testify of the Father and the Son to our minds and hearts. The Holy Ghost is a personage of spirit that speaks to our souls and by its power we are able to understand and live the gospel of Jesus Christ.

Everyone in the world can feel the influence of the Holy Ghost at certain times; however, the *gift* of the Holy Ghost is the privilege to receive its constant companionship and guidance by the laying on of hands. The gift of the Holy Ghost is bestowed upon a repentant person whose sins have been washed away at baptism. To hear the quiet promptings of the Holy Ghost we must be obedient, humble, and prayerful. This great gift from a loving Father can bless us with guidance, comfort, and testimony.

QUOTES

↳ "The simplicity of this ordinance may cause us to overlook its significance. These four words—*Receive the Holy Ghost*—are not a passive pronouncement; rather, they constitute a priesthood injunction—an authoritative admonition to act and not simply to be acted upon." (David A. Bednar, "Receive the Holy Ghost," *Ensign*, Nov. 2010.)

↳ "We need the help of the Holy Ghost if we are to make our way safely through what the Apostle Paul called the 'perilous times' in which we now live." (Gerald N. Lund, "Opening Our Hearts," *Ensign*, Apr. 2008.)

↳ "When the Prophet Joseph Smith was asked 'wherein [the LDS Church] differed . . . from the other religions of the day,' he replied that it was in 'the gift of the Holy Ghost by the laying on of hands, . . . [and] that all other considerations were contained in the gift of the Holy Ghost.' " (James E. Faust, "The Light in their Eyes," *Ensign*, Nov. 2005.)

↳ "The Holy Ghost . . . is our comforter, our direction finder, our communicator, our interpreter, our witness, and our purifier—our infallible guide and sanctifier." (Dallin H. Oaks, "Always Have His Spirit," *Ensign*, Nov. 1996.)

↳ "Testimony brings to us a knowledge that the gospel is true, but conversion by the Spirit brings something more." (Loren C. Dunn, "Fire and the Holy Ghost," *Ensign*, June 1995.)

↳ "If [we] would open [our] hearts to the refining influence of this unspeakable gift of the Holy Ghost, a glorious new spiritual dimension would come to light." (Joseph B. Wirthlin, "The Unspeakable Gift," *Ensign*, May 2003.)

GOSPEL ART

Boy Samuel Called by the Lord (18 GAB)
The Liahona (61 GAB)
Abinadi before King Noah (75 GAB)
Enos Praying (72 GAB)
Samuel the Lamanite on the Wall (81 GAB)
The Gift of the Holy Ghost (105 GAB)
John the Baptist Baptizing Jesus (35 GAB)

VIDEOS

"The Unspeakable Gift of the Holy Ghost": www.lds.org/media-library
/video/2012-01-0010-the-unspeakable-gift-of-the-holy-ghost

"Feeling the Holy Ghost": www.lds.org/media-library/video/2012-01-001
-feeling-the-holy-ghost

"Having the Holy Ghost": www.lds.org/media-library/video/2012-01-005
-having-the-holy-ghost

There is an excellent 3-part series called "Patterns of Light" by Elder
Bednar at: www.lds.org/media-library/video/2012-01-011-patterns-of
-light-discerning-light

ARTICLES

Douglas L. Callister, "Seeking the Spirit of God," *Ensign* Nov. 2000.

Neal A. Maxwell, "The Holy Ghost: Glorifying Christ," *Ensign*, July 2002.

James E. Faust, "Communion with The Holy Spirit," *Ensign*, Mar. 2002.

Loren C. Dunn, "Fire and the Holy Ghost," *Ensign*, June 1995.

Boyd K. Packer, "The Gift of the Holy Ghost: What Every Member Should
Know," *Ensign*, Aug. 2006.

David A. Bednar, "That We May Always Have His Spirit to Be with Us,"
Ensign, May 2006.

James E. Faust, "The Gift of the Holy Ghost—A Sure Compass," *Ensign*, Apr.
1996.

OBJECT LESSONS

- Have the class listen to the voices of apostles and prophets and try to guess
whose voices they are. Then play some voices of members of their family.
Talk about how it is much easier to recognize a voice when you are familiar with it. We need to spend time in the scriptures and in prayer in order
to recognize the voice of the Lord through the Holy Ghost.

- Show the class a variety of objects that involve air in some way: balloons,
a bicycle tire, hair dryer, inflatable balls, air pump, aerosol can, fan, soap
bubbles, etc. Ask the class what they have in common. Explain that while
we can't see air, we know it's there because of the affects it has on each
of those objects. We can't see the Holy Ghost because He doesn't have a
physical body, but we can feel His power and influence.

- ↝ Put a pile of cushions on the floor with a dried pea hidden underneath. Get some volunteers to sit on the cushions and guess what is hidden underneath. You can even tell the class the story about the princess and the pea. The Holy Ghost makes us more sensitive to spiritual things. We are truly sons and daughters of a king.

- ↝ Demonstrate the difference between the Holy Ghost and the *gift* of the Holy Ghost by using a flashlight. Everyone in the world can feel flashes of inspiration from the Holy Ghost at times when they are receiving comfort, guidance, or a witness of truth; however, it often quickly fades away. Make the flashlight go on and off. After you are baptized and given the *gift* of the Holy Ghost, you have the privilege of having the Holy Ghost as a constant companion. Turn on the flashlight and keep it on. We can keep our spiritual "batteries" charged and receive continuous light from the Holy Ghost if we live worthily.

- ↝ Show a laptop computer and explain that it has a special device inside that allows it to pick up an internet signal. If the computer is in range of the signal, it has the ability to receive information from all over the world. As baptized members of the church we have also been given a special device: the Holy Ghost. When we are in spiritual range we can receive information from heaven! Talk about some of the things that help us stay in range, as well as those things that keep us from it.

- ↝ Before the class begins, put water in a clear glass and put some hydrogen peroxide in another clear glass. They should look the same to your class. Ask for a volunteer to dip his or her index fingers on each hand into the two glasses. Now ask the volunteer to rub his or her fingers with each separate hand until the dipping fingers are dry. One should look the same, while the other one should have some white streaks on it (from the hydrogen peroxide). Ask the class "What is the chemical formula for water?" (H_2O). "What is the chemical formula for hydrogen peroxide?" (H_2O_2). How much difference does one oxygen molecule make? The water represents how we can all feel the Holy Ghost at certain times in our lives. The hydrogen peroxide shows how the *gift* of the Holy Ghost can stay with you.

• •

CHALLENGE

D&C 8:2 gives us a pattern the Lord uses to help us recognize the Holy Ghost: "Yea, behold, I will tell you in your mind and in your heart, by the Holy Ghost, which shall come upon you and which shall dwell in your heart."

Begin a "spiritual journal" where you record your spiritual experiences when you felt the Holy Ghost in your life.

. . . .

DOCTRINAL MASTERY PASSAGES

- 2 Nephi 32:3
- Moroni 10:4–5
- James 1:5–6

- D&C 8:2–3
- D&C 130:22–23

. . . .

PREACH MY GOSPEL

18, 90–91

. . . .

NOTES

Prayer

MUSIC

"Before Thee, Lord, I Bow My Head," *Hymns*, no. 158
"Did You Think to Pray?" *Hymns*, no. 140
"Prayer Is the Soul's Sincerest Desire," *Hymns*, no. 145
"Sweet Hour of Prayer," *Hymns*, no. 142
"A Child's Prayer," *Children's Songbook*, 12
"Joseph Smith's First Prayer," *Hymns*, no. 26

SUMMARY

Prayer is the vehicle we can use to communicate with our Father in Heaven. We are commanded to pray always unto the Father and only Him. We can pray either vocally or silently, asking for guidance and strength, confessing our sins, showing gratitude, and requesting specific blessings. We should pray individually and as families each day. God answers our prayers by granting us increased ability or by inspiring others to help us. As we pray, we draw closer to our Heavenly Father until His will is the same as ours.

One of the most powerful truths we can know is that the Creator of the universe knows and loves us personally. Prayer enables us to talk to our Father who is in heaven as if He were speaking with us face to face here on earth. How wonderful it is, not only that God truly hears our prayers, but that He wants to hear them. Inspired lives included daily personal prayer, family prayer, and, if we are married, companionship prayer. Those prayers should be filled with active listening

QUOTES

- "Prayer is a supernal gift of our Father in Heaven to every soul. Think of it: the absolute Supreme Being, the most all-knowing, all-seeing, all-powerful personage, encourages you and me, as insignificant as we are, to converse with Him as our Father." (Richard G. Scott, "Using the Supernal Gift of Prayer," *Ensign,* May 2007.)

- "A key to improved prayer is to learn to ask the right questions. Consider changing from asking for the things you want to honestly seeking what He wants for you. Then as you learn His will, pray that you will be led to have the strength to fulfill it." (Richard G. Scott, "Using the Supernal Gift of Prayer," *Ensign*, May 2007.)

- "Our Father in Heaven has promised us peace in times of trial and has provided a way for us to come to Him in our need. He has given us the privilege and power of prayer." (Rex D. Pinegar, "Peace through Prayer," *Ensign,* May 1993, 65–68.)

- "Men and women of integrity, character, and purpose have ever recognized a power higher than themselves and have sought through prayer to be guided by such power." (Thomas S. Monson, "The Prayer of Faith," *Ensign*, Aug. 1995.)

· ·

GOSPEL ART

Jesus Praying in Gethsemane (56 GAB)
Enos Praying (72 GAB)
Moroni Hides the Plates in the Hill Cumorah (86 GAB)
The First Vision (90 GAB)
Young Boy Praying (GAB)
Family Prayer (112 GAB)
Daniel in the Lions' Den (26 GAB)

· ·

VIDEOS

"Pray Often": www.lds.org/manual/preach-my-gospel/asl/chapter3/lesson4 #pray-often

"Pray in Your Families": www.lds.org/media-library/video/2012-08-2900 -pray-in-your-families

"Pray with Faith": www.lds.org/manual/preach-my-gospel/asl/chapter4

"And My Soul Hungered": www.lds.org/media-library/video/2012-08
-1710-and-my-soul-hungered
"How God Talks to Us Today": www.lds.org/media-library/video/2010
-05-1120-how-god-talks-to-us-today

* *

ARTICLES

David A. Bednar, "Pray Always," *Ensign*, Nov. 2008.
Dallin H. Oaks, "The Language of Prayer," *Ensign*, May 1993.
Russell M. Nelson, "Lessons from the Lord's Prayers," *Ensign*, May 2009.
James E. Faust, "The Lifeline of Prayer," *Ensign*, May 2002.
N. Eldon Tanner, "Importance and Efficacy of Prayer," *Ensign*, Aug. 1971.
Spencer W. Kimball, "Pray Always," *Ensign*, Oct. 1981.

* *

OBJECT LESSONS

↪ Invite the class to share their experiences of finding a moment in their
hectic lives for personal prayer. Before the discussion, ask a volunteer in
private to keep raising her hand while you ignore her. You could even
acknowledge her but tell her you need to say a few more things before she
can talk. Finally, when you call on her have her tell the class of your plan
and explain that sometimes our prayers are like that; we do all of the talking and don't let the Lord participate in the discussion!

↪ As you walk into the room, talk loudly on your mobile phone as if you are
talking to a friend. Talk about your plans for the day, the things you need
to do, and then ask for advice. Ask the class to compare your conversation to prayer. Remind them that talking on a cell phone is different from
prayer in the following ways:

> » God is never out of range
> » We never "lose the signal"
> » The battery never runs dead
> » We never run out of minutes
> » We don't have to remember God's number . . . just talk!

↪ Show a letter that is addressed to someone, but doesn't have a postage
stamp on it and ask the class why the postman won't deliver it. Read
Alma 33:11 and ask why the prayer of Zenos was heard? Explain that the

postage stamp represents sincerity. Sincerity is the postage that delivers our letter (prayer) to Heavenly Father.

- Ask the class to take several long deep breaths. There are interesting breathing exercises you can find online you could have the members do for a few minutes. We need to breathe to stay alive. When we breathe, we inhale oxygen and exhale carbon dioxide. Breathing actually cleanses us. Just as breathing can bring cleansing to our physical bodies, so can prayer to our spiritual bodies. Prayer can be a lot like breathing. We need to pray to stay spiritually alive. Paul states in 1 Thessalonians 5:17 that we are to "pray without ceasing." We can't live if our breathing ceases. We need to connect with God in prayer. It is essential to our spiritual health and survival!

CHALLENGE

Say a prayer today without asking for anything; just give thanks to the Lord. Offer another prayer tomorrow, focusing on other people's needs and how you could help them. Don't mention any of your needs. (Heavenly Father already knows about them anyway!) Write in your journal about those two conversations with Heavenly Father.

DOCTRINAL MASTERY PASSAGES

- 2 Nephi 32:8–9
- James 1:5–6
- D&C 8:2–3
- D&C 10:5
- D&C 25:12

PREACH MY GOSPEL

38, 73, 93–95

NOTES

_____

_____

The Sacrament

MUSIC

"In Memory of the Crucified," *Hymns*, no. 190
"While of These Emblems We Partake," *Hymns*, no. 173–174
"He Died! The Great Redeemer Died," *Hymns*, no. 192
"God Loved Us, So He Sent His Son," *Hymns*, no. 187
"Again We Meet Around the Board," *Hymns*, no. 186
"Father in Heaven, We Do Believe," *Hymns*, no. 180
"We'll Sing All Hail to Jesus' Name," *Hymns*, no. 182

SUMMARY

The sacrament is an ordinance designed by the Lord to help us remember His atoning sacrifice and the hope we have in Him of returning to live with our Father in Heaven. It is full of rich symbolism and offers an opportunity to renew our baptismal covenants, which also incorporate the same symbols.

The bread represents the Savior's body, which was ransomed for us on the cross and later resurrected in glory. The wine (water) causes our mind to reflect on the blood, which was shed for our sins and by which we are atoned for our sins. By partaking of the sacrament each week at church, we are remembering our covenants and that through Christ, we too can overcome physical and spiritual death.

When the bread and water trays are placed on the wooden table at church with the white tablecloth carefully draped over them, they symbolically represent Christ on the wooden cross, and later of His linen-covered body in the tomb. The sacrament is a powerful image of the Atonement of Jesus Christ.

QUOTES

- "The Spirit heals and renews our souls. The promised blessing of the sacrament is that we will 'always have his Spirit to be with us.' " (Cheryl A. Esplin, "The Sacrament – a Renewal for the Soul," *Ensign*, Oct. 2014.)
- "When we partake of the sacrament with a sincere heart, with real intent, forsaking our sins, and renewing our commitment to God, the Lord provides a way whereby sins can be forgiven." (Vaughn J. Featherstone, "Sacrament Meeting and the Sacrament," *Ensign,* Sept. 2001, 23–25.)
- "As we worthily partake of the sacrament, we will sense those things we need to improve in and receive the help and determination to do so. No matter what our problems, the sacrament always gives hope." (John H. Groberg, "The Beauty and Importance of the Sacrament," *Ensign,* May 1989, 38–40.)
- "Reminding us weekly of our need to foster charity toward our fellow Saints, the sacrament can be a great force for unity in our congregations." (John S. Tanner, "Reflections on the Sacrament Prayers," *Ensign,* Apr. 1986, 7–11.)
- As we partake of the sacrament, "our witness that we are willing to take upon us the name of Jesus Christ constitutes our declaration of candidacy for exaltation in the celestial kingdom." (Dallin H. Oaks, "Taking upon Us the Name of Jesus Christ," *Ensign,* May 1985, 80–83.

GOSPEL ART

Jesus Washing the Apostles' Feet (55 GAB)
Jesus Praying in Gethsemane (56 GAB)
The Crucifixion (57 GAB)
Burial of Jesus (58 GAB)
Mary and the Resurrected Jesus Christ (59 GAB)
Jesus Shows His Wounds (60 GAB)
Jesus at the Door (65 GAB)
Jesus Christ (1 GAB)
The Empty Tomb (245 GAB)
Blessing the Sacrament (107 GAB)
Passing the Sacrament (108 GAB)

VIDEOS

"Sacrament of the Lord's Supper": www.lds.org/media-library/video/2011
-03-042-sacrament-of-the-lords-supper

"Sacredness of the Sacrament": www.lds.org/media-library/video/2012-06
-1370-sacredness-of-the-sacrament

"The Emblems of the Sacrament": www.lds.org/media-library/video/2013
-10-1180-the-emblems-of-the-sacrament

"The Sacrament—A Renewal for the Soul": www.lds.org/media-library
/video/2014-10-140-sister-cheryl-a-esplin-highlights

"Sacrament Worship": www.lds.org/media-library/video/2012-05-8430
-sacrament-worship

ARTICLES

L. Tom Perry, "As Now We Take the Sacrament," *Ensign*, May 2006.

Dallin H. Oaks, "Sacrament Meeting and the Sacrament," *Ensign*, Nov. 2008.

Russell M. Nelson, "Worshiping at Sacrament Meeting," *Ensign*, Aug. 2004.

David B. Haight, "The Sacrament—and the Sacrifice," *Ensign*, Nov. 1989.

David B. Haight, "Remembering the Savior's Atonement," *Ensign*, April 1988.

OBJECT LESSONS

- Prepare a pane of clear glass or picture frame that is dirty on one side and show it to the class. Sometimes we don't even realize how dirty we're getting from the world (inside and out) because it accumulates over time. Use a glass cleaner to clear away some of the dirt on the glass. By coming to church and partaking of the sacrament, we can become unspotted from the world and have clearer vision. Read D&C 59:9 to the class.
- Pass out a basket with four different kinds of candy in it. After the members have selected their candy, divide them into 4 groups based on candy type. Each group will then be given a different topic to discuss:
    1. What do you do to help you focus on the Savior during sacrament meeting?
    2. How do you help your children keep the Sabbath Day holy and make the sacrament meaningful to them?
    3. Should children before the age of eight partake of the sacrament

even though they have not yet been baptized and, therefore, aren't renewing their covenants when they take the bread and water?

4. What do you do to "always remember Him" during the week?

- Sing one verse from each of the suggested hymns for this lesson (listed above). Music always invites the Spirit into a room in such a beautiful way.
- Invite some of the young men in the ward who have taken the sacrament to homebound members to share their experiences about that loving act of service.

CHALLENGE

Pass out cards where the class members can write down things they want to think about during the sacrament. Offer suggestions for quotes or scriptures they could write on their card. Encourage them to refer to those cards next Sunday when the sacrament is being passed.

DOCTRINAL MASTERY PASSAGES

- 2 Nephi 32:8–9
- Mosiah 3:19
- Alma 34:32–34
- Isaiah 1:18
- Isaiah 53:3–5
- John 3:5
- John 14:15
- John 17:3
- 1 Corinthians 15:20–22
- D&C 19:16–19
- D&C 58:42–43
- D&C 59:9–10

PREACH MY GOSPEL

9, 63, 64, 74

NOTES

_____

_____

_____

Testimony

MUSIC

"Go Forth with Faith," *Hymns*, no. 263
"Faith of Our Fathers," *Hymns*, no. 84
"When Faith Endures," *Hymns*, no. 128
"True to the Faith," *Hymns*, no. 254
"Come Unto Jesus," *Hymns*, no. 117

SUMMARY

As we exercise faith in the Lord, live His commandments, and pray for under-standing, we gain a testimony. Elder Dallin H. Oaks described a testimony as "a personal witness borne to our souls by the Holy Ghost that certain facts of eternal significance are true and that we know them to be true" ("Testimony," *Ensign*, May 2008). As we live gospel principles, we test them in our lives and gain knowledge that they are true and have blessed our lives.

As life presents challenges, our testimony can waver; therefore, it is vital that we nurture it each day with prayer, scripture study, and faith. Attending church meetings weekly can give us much needed strength as we hear the tes-timonies of others and learn how to better apply gospel principles to our lives. Participating in ordinances in the temple can provide peace to our souls as we try to overcome our doubts and trials.

QUOTES

⇀ "Honestly acknowledge your questions and your concerns, but first and forever fan the flame of your faith, because all things are possible to them that believe." (Jeffrey R. Holland, " 'Lord, I Believe,' " *Ensign*, May 2013.)

- "It is not enough to know that God lives, that Jesus Christ is our Savior, and that the gospel is true. We must take the high road by acting upon that knowledge." (Dallin H. Oaks, "Be Not Deceived," *Ensign*, Nov. 2004, 46.)
- "This is my prayer for all of us—'Lord, increase our faith.' Increase our faith to bridge the chasms of uncertainty and doubt. . . . Grant us faith to look beyond the problems of the moment to the miracles of the future. . . . Give us faith to do what is right and let the consequence follow." (Gordon B. Hinckley, "Lord, Increase Our Faith," *Ensign,* Nov. 1987.)
- "We promote the process of strengthening our faith when we do what is right—increased faith always follows." (L. Whitney Clayton, "Help Thou Mine Unbelief," *Ensign,* Nov. 2001.)
- "Faith in Jesus Christ takes us beyond mere acceptance of the Savior's identity and existence. It includes having complete confidence in His infinite and eternal redemptive power." (James O. Mason, "Faith in Jesus Christ," *Ensign,* Apr. 2001, 22–27.)

GOSPEL ART

Jesus Praying in Gethsemane (56 GAB)
The Crucifixion (57 GAB)
Jesus at the Door (65 GAB)
Jesus the Christ (1 GAB)
Enos Praying (72 GAB)
Conversion of Alma the Younger (77 GAB)
The Ten Commandments (14 GAB)
Abraham Taking Isaac to Be Sacrificed (9 GAB)
Three Men in the Fiery Furnace (25 GAB)
Daniel in the Lions' Den (26 GAB)
Moses and the Brass Serpent (16 GAB)
Christ Healing a Blind Man (42 GAB)
Jesus Blessing Jairus's Daughter (41 GAB)
Two Thousand Young Warriors (80 GAB)
The Brother of Jared Sees the Finger of the Lord (85 GAB)

VIDEOS

"The Transforming Power of Faith and Character," Richard G. Scott: www.lds.org/media-library/video/2015-00-006-transforming-power -of-faith-and-character?lang=eng&category=social-media-sharable-videos

"We Believe: Theme Song": www.lds.org/media-library/video/2010-12-02 -we-believe-theme-song

"Finding Faith in Christ": www.lds.org/media-library/video/2004-01-01 -finding-faith-in-christ

"Waiting on Our Road to Damascus": www.lds.org/media-library/video /2012-01-003-waiting-on-our-road-to-damascus

• •

ARTICLES

Gordon B. Hinckley, "Faith: The Essence of True Religion," *Ensign*, Oct.1995.

Russell M. Nelson, "Faith in Jesus Christ," *Ensign*, Mar. 2008.

Robert D. Hales, "Finding Faith in the Lord Jesus Christ," *Ensign*, Nov. 2004.

Robert D. Hales, "General Conference: Strengthening Faith and Testimony," *Ensign,* Nov. 2013.

Henry B. Eyring, "Testimony and Conversion," *Ensign*, Feb. 2015.

• •

OBJECT LESSONS

↬ Hold up a hymnbook with only three fingers. Talk about how you need three things to build a strong testimony: (1) prayer, (2) scriptures, (3) church attendance. What are more things you could do to have a strong testimony? Add a finger to hold up the hymnbook with each one you add. See how much more stable your spirituality is with ten fingers/things you do!

↬ At the end of this book is a listing of websites where you can get free clip art. Create a Family Home Evening Packet about faith and testimony that the class members can copy to take home and use with their families. Invite the class to color pictures and cut out visual aids for their packet while they listen to the lesson. Provide scissors, crayons, and markers.

↬ Show the class a checkerboard with 1 grain of wheat on the first square, 2 on the second, 4 on the third, and 8, 16, 32, 64, 128, etc. Ask the class, "At this rate of doubling every square, how much grain would you have on the checkerboard by the time you reach the 64th square?" Let the class guess and tell them the correct answer is enough grain to cover the entire subcontinent of India 50 feet deep! Each square represents some area of their life where they need to trust God. Talk about how our faith may start out small, but as God uses it, the end result can be miraculous and quite powerful!

↝ Pass out some baby food jars filled with whipping cream. Ask the class if they have faith that the cream can turn into butter. Explain that faith isn't just believing in something, but that it leads to action. Have the class shake the jars during the lesson until the cream turns into sweet butter. Talk about how building a testimony requires time, work, and patience. Before the lesson ends pass out blueberry muffins that the butter can be served on for all to enjoy.

CHALLENGE

Write a list of all the things that build your faith. Begin doing one of the things on your list that you haven't included in your daily life lately.

DOCTRINAL MASTERY PASSAGES

- 2 Nephi 2:27
- 2 Nephi 28:7–9
- Mosiah 4:30
- Alma 32:21
- Alma 34:32–34
- Alma 41:10
- Ether 12:6
- Genesis 39:9
- Exodus 20:3–17
- Psalms 24:3–4
- Proverbs 3:5–6
- Isaiah 1:18
- Isaiah 55:8–9
- John 14:15
- James 1:5–6
- James 2:17–18
- D&C 19:16–19
- D&C 58:42–43
- D&C 59:9–10
- D&C 82:3

PREACH MY GOSPEL

49–50, 62–63, 93–95, 155, 187–90, 195

NOTES

Testimony

Discipleship

MUSIC

"I Know That My Redeemer Lives," *Hymns*, no. 136
"Jesus, Lover of My Soul," *Hymns*, no. 102
"I'm Trying to Be Like Jesus" *Children's Songbook*, 78
"The Lord Is My Light," *Hymns*, no. 89
"Jesus, the Very Thought of Thee," *Hymns*, no. 141
"Come Unto Jesus," *Hymns*, no. 117

SUMMARY

What is at the center of our daily lives? More to the point, *who* is our life centered on? Our challenge during mortality is to choose the eternal kingdom of God rather than temporary earthly glory. What good is having someone who can walk on water if you don't follow in His footsteps?

Being a true disciple means that we choose to follow Him each day. We're certainly not perfect, but we can try our best to be more like Him in our thoughts, words, and actions. Learning to love and serve others makes us more like Christ than almost any other thing we can do.

QUOTES

↦ "The Christ-centered life produces in us, not a woeful countenance, but a disciplined enthusiasm to work righteousness." (Neal A. Maxwell, "The Christ-Centered Life," *Ensign*, Aug. 1981.)

↦ "I bear witness that obedience to the gospel plan is the only way to build a Christ-centered life." (Merrill J. Bateman, "Living a Christ-Centered Life," *Ensign*, Jan. 1999.)

➤ "In this, the dispensation of the fullness of time, as we prepare for the final satanic battles in anticipation of the return of Christ to the earth, it is very important to know who is on the Lord's side. The Lord needs to know on whom He can rely." (Robert C. Oaks, "Who's on the Lord's Side? Who?" *Ensign*, May 2005.)

➤ "If you will remain on the Lord's side of the line, the adversary cannot come there to tempt you." (Charles W. Dahlquist II, "Who's on the Lord's Side?", *Ensign*, May 2007.)

➤ "The Lord has left no doubt in defining His side and where the Saints should be in their thoughts, words, actions, and practices. We have His counsel in the scriptures and in the words of the prophets." (Joseph B. Wirthlin, "The Lord's Side," *Ensign*, Mar. 1993.)

➤ "To follow Christ is to become like Him. It is to learn from His character. As spirit children of our Heavenly Father, we do have the potential to incorporate Christlike attributes into our life and character." (Dieter F. Uchtdorf, "Developing Christlike Attributes," *Ensign*, Oct. 2008.)

• •

GOSPEL ART

Building the Ark (7 GAB)
Daniel Refusing the King's Meat and Wine (23 GAB)
Daniel in the Lions' Den (26 GAB)
Calling of the Fishermen (37 GAB)
Jesus Washing the Apostles' Feet (55 GAB)
Jesus at the Door (65 GAB)
Christ and the Rich Young Ruler (48 GAB)
Alma Baptizes in the Waters of Mormon (76 GAB)
Captain Moroni Raises the Title of Liberty (79 GAB)
Two Thousand Young Warriors (80 GAB)
Salt Lake Temple (119 GAB)
Latter-day Prophets (122–137 GAB)
Baptism (103, 104 GAB)
Young Boy Praying (111 GAB)
Family Prayer (112 GAB)
Young Couple Going to the Temple (120 GAB)
Isaiah Writes of Christ's Birth (22 GAB)
The Nativity (30 GAB)

Boy Jesus in the Temple (34 GAB)
John the Baptist Baptizing Jesus (35 GAB)
Sermon on the Mount (39 GAB)
Jesus Blessing Jairus's Daughter (41 GAB)
Mary and Martha (45 GAB)
Triumphal Entry (50 GAB)
Jesus Praying in Gethsemane (56 GAB)
The Crucifixion (57 GAB)
Burial of Jesus (58 GAB)
Mary and the Resurrected Lord (59 GAB)
Jesus Shows His Wounds (60 GAB)
Go Ye Therefore (61 GAB)
The Ascension of Jesus (62 GAB)
Jesus at the Door (65 GAB)
The Second Coming (66 GAB)
The Resurrected Jesus Christ (66 GAB)
Christ Walking on the Water (43 GAB)
Christ and the Rich Young Ruler (48 GAB)
Jesus Christ Appears to the Nephites (82 GAB)
Jesus Blesses the Nephite Children (84 GAB)

VIDEOS

"What Is Discipleship?": www.lds.org/media-library/video/2012-01-8620
-what-is-discipleship
"Choose This Day": www.lds.org/media-library/video/2009-09-37-choose
-this-day
"Answers to Life's Great Questions": www.lds.org/media-library/video/2009
-01-58-answers-to-lifes-great-questions

ARTICLES

Richard J. Maynes, "Establishing a Christ-Centered Home," *Ensign*, May
2011.
Lawrence E. Corbridge, "Valiant in the Testimony of Jesus Christ," *Ensign*,
September 2011.
Clate W. Mask Jr., "Standing Spotless before the Lord," *Ensign*, May 2004.
Stephen A. West, "Are You on the Lord's Side?" *New Era*, Sept. 2002.

Bernard P. Brockbank, "Knowing God," *Ensign,* July 1972, 121–23.

N. Eldon Tanner, "A Basis for Faith in the Living God," *Ensign,* Nov 1978, 46–49.

D. Todd Christofferson, "Reflections on a Consecrated Life," *Ensign,* Nov. 2010.

OBJECT LESSONS

- Get a picture of Jesus Christ where He is in the center and other items or people are surrounding him. Cut it up into puzzle pieces and invite the members to put it together. Notice that once you put Christ in the center, the rest of the picture puzzle is easier to solve.

- Show various pictures that represent sources of light: the sun, solar panel, flashlight, candle, porch light, spotlight, lighthouse, fireplace, night-light, etc. Talk about their unique purposes and then show a picture of the Savior. Compare and contrast what His purpose is.

- Show some objects to the class. Invite three volunteers to help you. Each of three volunteers picks one of the items to describe a gospel principle that relates to the item. Then ask the class what item symbolizes a disciple. Discuss!

CHALLENGE

Look at the list of Christlike qualities that are included on page 115 of *Preach My Gospel.* Evaluate how you are doing in developing those characteristics. Create a plan of action for how you will make Christ more central in your daily thoughts and actions. What changes can you make to focus more on the Savior? What experiences can strengthen your testimony? What goals could you set to become more Christlike in your thoughts, words, and actions?

DOCTRINAL MASTERY PASSAGES

- 1 Nephi 19:23
- 2 Nephi 32:3
- Jacob 2:18–19
- Helaman 5:12
- 3 Nephi 27:27
- Moroni 7:16–17
- Moroni 10:4–5
- Exodus 20:3–17
- Deuteronomy 7:3–4
- Joshua 24:15
- Job 19:25–26
- Proverbs 3:5–6
- Isaiah 53:3–5
- Isaiah 55:8–9
- Daniel 2:44–45

- Matthew 6:24
- Luke 24:36–39
- John 14:15
- John 17:3

- Ephesians 4:11–14
- Revelation 20:12–13
- Joseph Smith History 1:15–20

- D&C 14:7
- D&C 76:22–24
- D&C 137:7–10

PREACH MY GOSPEL

1, 5, 33, 37, 46, 48, 51–54, 60–61, 90, 105, 108, 115–16, 123–26, 198–99

NOTES

Joseph Smith & the Restoration of the Gospel

MUSIC

"The Sacred Grove," *Children's Songbook*, 87
"A Key Was Turned in Latter Days" (Women), *Hymns*, no. 310
"Joseph Smith's First Prayer," *Hymns*, no. 26
"The Day Dawn Is Breaking," *Hymns*, no. 52
"The Glorious Gospel Light Has Shone," *Hymns*, no. 283
"High on the Mountain Top," *Hymns*, no. 5

SUMMARY

After the Savior ascended into heaven, His Church and its ordinances and teachings were lost in their purity. Priesthood authority and correct doctrine were restored in 1830, when a prophet of God was again chosen. The Church of Jesus Christ of Latter-day Saints offers the fulness of the gospel to the world today and will never be destroyed.

The Book of Mormon provides us with additional scriptures that teach us the gospel of Jesus Christ and testify that He lives and has established His kingdom here on earth. The priesthood has been restored so that we can participate in saving ordinances and be blessed here on earth and in heaven. How wonderful to be a member of the Church of Jesus Christ!

QUOTES

- "Joseph the Prophet became the means, in God's providence, to restore the old truths of the everlasting gospel of Jesus Christ, the plan of salvation, which is older than the human race. It is true, also, that his teachings were new to the people of his day because they had apostatized from the truth—but the principles of the gospel are the oldest truths in existence. They were new to Joseph's generation, as they are in part to ours, because men had gone astray, been cast adrift, shifted hither and thither by every new wind of doctrine which cunning men—so called progressives—had advanced. This made the Prophet Joseph a restorer, not a destroyer, of old truths." (Joseph F. Smith, *Teachings of Presidents of the Church: Joseph F. Smith*, 18.)

- "We declare to the world that the fullness of the gospel of Jesus Christ has been restored to the earth." (L. Tom Perry, "The Message of the Restoration." *Ensign*, May 2007.)

- "The dawn of the dispensation of the fulness of times rose upon the world. All of the good, the beautiful, the divine of all previous dispensations was restored in this most remarkable season." (Gordon B. Hinckley, "The Dawning of a Brighter Day," *Ensign*, May 2004.)

- "The Lord permitted these few poorly armed and ill-clad men at Valley Forge and elsewhere to defeat a great army, a few against the many, but the few had on their side the Lord God of heaven, that gave them victory. And there came political liberty and religious liberty with it, all in preparation for the day when a young boy would come forth and would seek and make contact with the Lord and open the doors of heaven again." (Spencer W. Kimball, *Teachings of Spencer W. Kimball*, 1982, 403.)

GOSPEL ART

Brother Joseph (87 GAB)
Joseph Smith Seeks Wisdom in the Bible (89 GAB)
Joseph Smith Translating the Book of Mormon (92 GAB)
The Prophet Joseph Smith (122 GAB)
Latter-day Prophets (137 GAB)

The First Vision (90 GAB)
John the Baptist Conferring the Aaronic Priesthood (93 GAB)
Melchizedek Priesthood Restoration (94 GAB)
Kirtland Temple (117 GAB)
Nauvoo Illinois Temple (118 GAB)
Salt Lake Temple (119 GAB)
Temple Baptismal Font (121 GAB)
Young Couple Going to the Temple (120 GAB)

VIDEOS

"The Restoration": www.lds.org/media-library/video/2008-06-01-the-restoration
"The Apostasy and Restoration": www.lds.org/media-library/video/2016-02
    -0001-the-apostasy-and-restoration
"April: The Apostasy and the Restoration": www.lds.org/media-library
    /video/youth-curriculum/april-the-apostasy-and-the-restoration
"Restoration of the Priesthood": www.lds.org/media-library/video/2010
    -05-1130-restoration-of-the-priesthood?category=youth-curriculum
    /april-the-apostasy-and-the-restoration
"The Apostasy and the Restoration—What the Restoration Means
    for Me": www.lds.org/media-library/video/2012-10-004-the-apostasy
    -and-the-restoration-what-the-restoration-means-for-me?category=youth
    -curriculum/april-the-apostasy-and-the-restoration

ARTICLES

Dieter F. Uchtdorf, "Are You Sleeping Through the Restoration?" *Ensign*, May 2014.
L. Tom Perry, "The Message of the Restoration," *Ensign*, May 2007.
James E. Faust, "The Restoration of All Things," *Ensign*, May 2006.
Gordon B. Hinckley, "His Latter-day Kingdom Has Been Established," *Ensign*, May 1991.
Bruce R. McConkie, "The Lord God of the Restoration," *Ensign*, Nov. 1980.
Hugh W. Pinnock, "The Gospel Restored," *Ensign*, May 1980.
Jeffrey R. Holland, "This, The Greatest of All Dispensations," *Ensign*, July 2007.
Russell M. Nelson, "Thus Shall My Church Be Called," *Ensign*, May 1990.
D. Todd Christofferson, "Come to Zion," *Ensign*, Nov. 2008.

Henry B. Eyring, "The True and Living Church," *Ensign*, May 2008.
M. Russell Ballard, "The Truth of God Shall Go Forth," *Ensign*, Nov. 2008.

OBJECT LESSONS

- Play telephone! Give a long sentence to each row of brothers or sisters and then see which group is able to get the closest to the original by the end. Talk about unbroken lines and how they're similar to the restoration of gospel principles and the Church.
- Pass out gum to the class and tell them to chew it for about five minutes to get all of the flavor out of it. Now ask the class to put it back into the wrapper and mold it into the original form. Many men have tried to re-create Christ's true church. Only with the Savior's help was Joseph Smith able to restore the Lord's church.
- Show the class some tarnished silver and spoons. Talk about restoration of Christ's true church while you polish the silver. Discuss how the beauty was always there, but that no one could see it until it was restored. Isn't it interesting that a silversmith is someone who is trained to restore that beauty and the Prophet Joseph's name was Smith?
- Pass out pictures that illustrate major points of the talk(s) and invite the class to discuss each particular gospel truth and how our lives are enriched because of the correct knowledge we now have about it. It will naturally become a sweet testimony meeting.

CHALLENGE

Write down your specific testimony of each of the gospel principles that are featured in this lesson. Give examples from your life that illustrate how you learned that each principle is true.

DOCTRINAL MASTERY PASSAGES

- Moroni 10:4–5
- Exodus 33:11
- Joshua 1:8
- Joshua 24:15
- Jeremiah 16:16
- Ezekiel 37:15–17
- Daniel 2:44–45
- Amos 3:7
- Matthew 16:15–19
- Acts 7:55–56
- Ephesians 4:11–14
- Hebrews 5:4
- Joseph Smith History 1:15–20
- D&C 8:2–3

- D&C 84:33–39 • D&C 121:34–36 • 2 Thessalonians 2:1–3

• •

PREACH MY GOSPEL

1, 5, 6, 7, 31, 32, 34, 35, 36, 37, 44, 103–114

• •

NOTES

_____

_____

_____

_____

_____

_____

_____

_____

_____

_____

_____

_____

_____

_____

_____

_____

_____

_____

_____

_____

The Importance of Family

"Families Can Be Together Forever," *Hymns*, no. 300
"Home Can Be a Heaven on Earth," *Hymns*, no. 298
"I Am a Child of God," *Hymns*, no. 301
"O My Father," *Hymns*, no. 292
"Our Father, by Whose Name," *Hymns*, no. 296
"Teach Me to Walk in the Light," *Hymns*, no. 304

SUMMARY

Life is eternal. We come from heavenly parents who are waiting for us to return to Them, having learned the lessons of life and gained the characteristics They possess. To remind us of our heavenly home, we are given the opportunity to be parents here on earth and raise a family of our own. Salvation is a family affair. The family is the most important unit in time and eternity. We are placed here as families to learn how to care for one another, so that we may all safely return home together. Temple marriage is a covenant partnership with the Lord that allows us to seal souls together as eternal families.

Heavenly Father has placed us here on earth in families so that we can learn to work together and help one another return to our heavenly home, each one playing an important role. Fathers are to provide, protect, and preside over families. Mothers are divinely designed to bear and nurture children. Children are commanded to honor and obey their parents. If everyone takes

82

responsibility for a happy family, they can all experience a little bit of heaven on earth.

Be sensitive to the brothers and sisters in the class who may have never married, lost a spouse, or divorced. Remind them the Lord has promised a fulness of blessings to all those who are faithful.

QUOTES

- "In light of the ultimate purpose of the great plan of happiness, I believe that the ultimate treasures on earth and in heaven are our children and our posterity." (Dallin H. Oaks, "The Great Plan of Happiness," *Ensign,* Nov. 1993.)

- "Under the plan of heaven, the husband and the wife walk side by side as companions, neither one ahead of the other, but a daughter of God and a son of God walking side by side. Let your families be families of love and peace and happiness. Gather your children around you and have your family home evenings, teach your children the ways of the Lord, read to them from the scriptures, and let them come to know the great truths of the eternal gospel as set forth in these words of the Almighty." (Gordon B. Hinckley, "Selections from Addresses of President Gordon B. Hinckley, *Ensign,* Mar. 2001, 64.)

- "Our family is the focus of our greatest work and joy in this life; so will it be throughout all eternity." (Russell M. Nelson, "Set in Order Thy House," *Ensign,* Nov. 2001.)

- "The key to strengthening our families is having the Spirit of the Lord come into our homes. The goal of our families is to be on the strait and narrow path." (Robert D. Hales, "Strengthening Families: Our Sacred Duty," *Ensign,* May 1999.)

- "The family unit is fundamental not only to society and to the Church but to our hope for eternal life." (Henry B. Eyring, "The Family," *Ensign,* Feb. 1998.)

- "Individual progression is fostered in the family, which is central to the Creator's plan for the eternal destiny of His children." (Russell M. Nelson, "Salvation and Exaltation," *Ensign,* May 2008.)

GOSPEL ART

Jesus Christ (1 GAB)

Adam and Eve Kneeling at an Altar (4 GAB)
Adam and Eve Teaching Their Children (5 GAB)
Jacob Blessing His Sons (12 GAB)
Lehi's Dream (69 GAB)
Elijah Appearing in the Kirtland Temple (95 GAB)
Young Couple Going to the Temple (120 GAB)

VIDEOS

"Until We Meet Again": www.lds.org/media-library/video/2011-07-362-until
-we-meet-again

"The Blessings of the Temple": www.lds.org/media-library/video/2009-03
-10-the-blessings-of-the-temple

"Faith and Families": www.lds.org/media-library/video/topics/family

"Marriage and Divorce": www.lds.org/media-library/video/2009-07-28
-marriage-and-divorce

ARTICLES

Robert D. Hales, "The Eternal Family," *Ensign*, Nov. 1996, 64–67.
Henry B. Eyring, "The Family," *Ensign*, Feb. 1998, 10–18.
L. Tom Perry, "The Importance of the Family," *Ensign*, May 2003, 40–43.
Spencer W. Kimball, "Living the Gospel in the Home," *Ensign*, May 1978.
Spencer W. Kimball, "The Importance of Celestial Marriage," *Ensign*, Oct.
1979, 2–6.
Bruce C. Hafen, "Covenant Marriage," *Ensign*, Nov. 1996, 26–28.
F. Burton Howard, "Eternal Marriage," *Ensign*, May 2003, 92–94.

OBJECT LESSONS

➥ Get two large envelopes, one with a picture of a temple on the outside. Ask
a volunteer to place paper dolls inside the two envelopes, creating families
out of the pictures. Lick the envelope that has the picture of a temple on
the outside. Talk about life's challenges that can tear us apart and then
put the two envelopes upside down, shaking the contents around. The
family that has been sealed together will stay together, but the pictures of
the other family will all fall out of the envelope.

- Pass out copies of the "Proclamation on the Family" to give to everyone in the class and have them color and decorate them during your lesson.
- Place a candy bar on each side of the room. Invite two volunteers to come up and link arms, back to back. Tell them they have ten seconds to get their respective candy bar. When you say "Go!" they will each begin pulling the other one in the opposite direction; one will either get their candy bar or neither will. Our goal as a family is to return to our heavenly home intact and it will take all of us working together to accomplish it.
- Place a stalk of celery in a glass of colored water a few days prior to your lesson. The food coloring in the water will actually draw up into the celery! Show the class your visual aid and ask them to draw analogies between the celery, food coloring, and our parenting skills. Children literally soak up what is around them in the home: anger, love, gospel study, apathy, etc. We need to constantly expose our children to positive behaviors in order for them to absorb the gospel.

CHALLENGE

Write down the names of everyone in your family. Write a list of things you can do to serve them and help them reach their personal goals.

DOCTRINAL MASTERY PASSAGES

- Ether 12:27
- Moroni 7:45
- 2 Timothy 3:1–5
- D&C 14:7
- D&C 58:26–27
- D&C 88:123–24
- D&C 131:1–4

PREACH MY GOSPEL

3, 32, 85, 159–64

NOTES

Choices & Consequences

MUSIC

"Dare to Do Right," *Children's Songbook*, 158
"Choose the Right," *Hymns*, no. 239
"Teach Me to Walk in the Light," *Hymns*, no. 304
"Who's on the Lord's Side?" *Hymns*, no. 260

SUMMARY

The right to choose between good and evil and to act for ourselves is called agency. It is a principle that existed before we came to earth and will continue to exist after we leave it. By following Jesus Christ, we are choosing eternal life and liberty. If we follow Satan we are selecting evil and eternal captivity. One of the purposes of mortality is to show which choices we'll make and so there must be opposition in all things in order for us to exercise agency.

While we are free to make choices, we are not free to choose the consequences of our actions. What good is having someone who can walk on water if you don't follow in His footsteps?

QUOTES

- "Modern revelation makes it clear that agency is a gift from our Heavenly

Father to allow us to choose obedience, which leads us to eternal life." (L. Lionel Kendrick, "Our Moral Agency," *Ensign*, Mar. 1996, 28–32.)

- ↦ "While the freedom to choose involves the risk of mistakes, it also offers the opportunity, through our Father's plan, to overcome them." (Spencer J. Condie, "Agency: The Gift of Choices," *Ensign,* Sept. 1995, 16–22.)
- ↦ "We are given the knowledge, the help, the enticement, and the freedom to choose the path of eternal safety and salvation. The choice to do so is ours." (Howard W. Hunter, "The Golden Thread of Choice," *Ensign,* Nov. 1989, 17–18.)
- ↦ "Ever and always [the Atonement] offers amnesty from transgression and from death if we will but repent. . . . Repentance is the key with which we can unlock the prison from inside . . . and agency is ours to use it." (Boyd K. Packer, "Atonement, Agency, Accountability," *Ensign,* May 1988, 69–72.)

GOSPEL ART

Ruth Gleaning in the Fields (17 GAB)
The Lord Created All Things (2 GAB)
Building the Ark (7 GAB)
Calling of the Fishermen (37 GAB)
The Sermon on the Mount (39 GAB)
The Good Samaritan (44 GAB)
Mary and Martha (45 GAB)
Parable of the Ten Virgins (53 GAB)
Go Ye Therefore (61 GAB)
Jesus Carrying a Lost Lamb (64 GAB)
Jesus at the Door (65 GAB)
Lehi's Dream (69 GAB)
Enos Praying (72 GAB)
Captain Moroni Raises the Title of Liberty (79 GAB)
Two Thousand Young Warriors (80 GAB)
The Brother of Jared Sees the Finger of the Lord (85 GAB)
Brother Joseph (87 GAB)
Joseph Smith Seeks Wisdom in the Bible (89 GAB)
Joseph Smith Translating the Book of Mormon (92 GAB)
Emma Crossing the Ice (96 GAB)
The Foundation of the Relief Society (98 GAB)
Handcart Pioneers Approaching the Salt Lake Valley (102 GAB)

Service (115 GAB)
Young Couple Going to the Temple (120 GAB)

• •

VIDEOS

"Act for Themselves": www.lds.org/media-library/video/2012-08-1260-act
-for-themselves

"Can you Imagine?": www.lds.org/media-library/video/2010-06-04-can-you
-imagine

"The Freedom To . . . ": www.lds.org/media-library/video/2009-06-27-the
-freedom-to

"Individual Agency": www.lds.org/media-library/video/2012-08-1410
-individual-agency

• •

ARTICLES

Robert D. Hales, "To Act for Ourselves: The Gift and Blessings of Agency,"
Ensign, May 2006.

Wolfgang H. Paul, "The Gift of Agency," *Ensign*, May 2006.

Howard W. Hunter, "The Golden Thread of Choice," *Ensign*, November 1989.

Delbert L. Stapley, "Using Our Free Agency," *Ensign*, May 1975.

Boyd K. Packer, "Atonement, Agency, Accountability," *Ensign*, May 1988.

Spencer J. Condie, "Agency: The Gift of Choices," *Ensign*, September 1995.

• •

OBJECT LESSONS

↦ Give a volunteer a bag marked "Good Choices" (filled with Legos). Give
another volunteer a second bag marked "Bad Choices" (filled with broken
sticks). Ask them to build the best house they can with what they were
given. Talk about how it's difficult to build a good life out of bad choices.

↦ Play a game of Jeopardy. You can create categories such as "Chapel Chat-
ter," "Gospel Gems," "Of Maps and Men," "Doctrinal Mastery Passages,"
etc. Divide the class into teams and let them choose categories and questions. You can get questions and answers online for Bible Trivia at www.
christianity.com/trivia/jeopardy.

• •

CHALLENGE

Our lives are ridiculously full and busy. Each day we choose what is most important to us by the things we fill our life with, whether intentionally or not. Make a list of all of the tasks you need to complete every day. Do those things bring you closer or farther from God? What things can you let go of? What new items could you add to show you choose righteousness over wickedness?

• •

DOCTRINAL MASTERY PASSAGES

- 1 Nephi 3:7
- 2 Nephi 2:27
- 2 Nephi 28:7–9
- Jacob 2:18–19
- Mosiah 3:19
- Mosiah 4:30
- Alma 34:32–34
- Alma 41:10
- Helaman 5:12
- Moroni 7:16–17
- Moroni 7:45
- Exodus 20:3–17
- Joshua 1:8
- Isaiah 1:18
- Matthew 6:24
- John 7:17
- John 14:15
- 1 Corinthians 10:13
- Revelation 20:12–13
- D&C 1:37–38
- D&C 14:7
- D&C 58:26–27

• •

PREACH MY GOSPEL

47–49, 66, 72, 75, 88, 150–51

• •

NOTES

_____

_____

_____

_____

_____

_____

_____

Fourth Sunday

Special Topics Chosen by General Church Leaders

The Sabbath Day

. . . .

MUSIC

"Sabbath Day," *Hymns*, no. 148
"Gently Raise the Sacred Strain," *Hymns*, no. 146
"We Meet, Dear Lord," *Hymns*, no. 151
"O Thou Kind and Gracious Father," *Hymns*, no. 150
"Welcome, Welcome, Sabbath Morning," *Hymns*, no. 280

. . . .

SUMMARY

God ordained the Sabbath day to be kept holy and declared it to be a day of rest from our labors. The Sabbath occurs every seven days and is designed to direct our thoughts away from the world and to focus on the Lord instead. In the beginning, God consecrated the seventh day to represent God's day of rest after He created the world. After Christ's Resurrection, the first day of the week was honored as the Sabbath to commemorate His Resurrection and symbolize how it is the Savior who truly gives us rest.

A helpful guideline in determining whether an activity is appropriate for the Sabbath is to ask the following questions: Will it draw me closer to God? Does it show respect and love for the Savior? Will it inspire me and direct my thoughts to the Lord? The Sabbath day is an opportunity to show the Lord that we put Him first in our lives. The fourth commandment helps us to remember our covenants and reevaluate our priorities and weekly activities.

. . . .

QUOTES

➵ "Now is the time to ask ourselves: Is the Sabbath a holy day or a holiday?

Shall I worship the Lord or worship pleasures and recreation?" (Charles Didier, "The Sabbath—Holy Day or Holiday?" *Ensign*, Oct. 1994, 26–31.)

- ☞ "Observance of the Sabbath is not a restriction but a source of strength and protection." (D. Kelly Ogden, "Remember the Sabbath Day," *Ensign*, Apr. 1994, 46–51.)
- ☞ "Our observance of the Sabbath is an indication of the depth of our conversion and our willingness to keep sacred covenants." (Earl C. Tingey, "The Sabbath Day and Sunday Shopping," *Ensign,* May 1996, 10–12.)
- ☞ "There is a sure protection for ourselves and our children against the plague of our day. The key to that sure protection surprisingly can be found in Sabbath observance." (James E. Faust, "The Lord's Day," *Ensign,* Nov. 1991, 33–35.)

GOSPEL ART

The Lord Created All Things (2 GAB)
Adam and Eve Kneeling at an Altar (4 GAB)
Adam and Eve Teaching Their Children (5 GAB)
The Ten Commandments (14 GAB)
Esther (21 GAB)
Jesus Praying with His Mother (33 GAB)
Mary and Martha (45 GAB)
Lehi's Dream (69 GAB)
Enos Praying (72 GAB)
Blessing the Sacrament (107 GAB)
Passing the Sacrament (108 GAB)
Family Prayer (112 GAB)

VIDEOS

"The Sabbath Is a Delight": https://www.lds.org/media-library/video/2015-12-008-the-sabbath-is-a-delight

"Upon My Holy Day—Honoring the Sabbath": https://www.lds.org/media-library/video/2016-10-0002-upon-my-holy-day-honoring-the-sabbath?category=prophets-and-apostles/prophets-and-apostles-sub-category

"Upon My Holy Day—Rest and Renewal": https://www.lds.org/media-library/video/2016-10-0003-upon-my-holy-day-rest-and-renewal

?category=prophets-and-apostles/prophets-and-apostles-sub
-category

· ·

ARTICLES

Ezra Taft Benson, "Keeping the Sabbath Day Holy," *Ensign*, May 1971.

H. Aldridge Gillespie, "The Blessing of Keeping the Sabbath Day Holy," *Ensign*, Nov. 2000.

John H. Groberg, "The Power of Keeping the Sabbath Day Holy," *Ensign*, Nov. 1984.

James E. Faust, "The Lord's Day," *Ensign*, Nov. 1991.

Earl C. Tingey, "Keeping the Sabbath Day Holy," *Ensign*, Feb. 2000.

Charles Didier, "The Sabbath—Holy Day or Holiday?" *Ensign*, Oct. 1994.

· ·

OBJECT LESSONS

⊸ Invite someone in the class to enjoy an ice cream sundae with you. Dish out some ice cream and comment on how excited everyone looks about the yummy treat. Now put on various toppings such as pepperoni, BBQ sauce, chopped onions, and grated cheese. The class will probably express disgust. Ask them why they don't want those toppings. They'll probably say that they like those ingredients, but not on top of a sundae. Talk about how choosing activities appropriate for Sunday is the same: activities we do during the week aren't bad activities, but they just may not be appropriate for the Sabbath day.

⊸ Ask for a volunteer to put some white sugar into a clear glass, representing the Sabbath Day (clean and white). Now ask him or her to add some hot chocolate mix on top, representing the rest of the week. The class will see a definite line, dividing the two colors. Now ask the student to mix them up together. The Lord asks us to set apart the Sabbath Day to make it different than the rest of the week. The Lord's day should look and feel different from the rest of our week.

⊸ Display a battery-operated flashlight with a weak battery. Talk about how ineffective it is and explain that when our spiritual batteries are recharged every week on the Sabbath our eternal vision is brighter.

· ·

CHALLENGE

Write a list with your family about all of the things you CAN do on the Sabbath day in order to keep the Lord's day holy. Focus on what makes Sunday different and special rather than all of the things you can't or shouldn't do. Fill your day with things that draw you closer to the Savior and build your testimony.

· ·

DOCTRINAL MASTERY PASSAGES

- Isaiah 58:13–14
- Exodus 19:5–6
- Joshua 24:15
- Exodus 20:3–17
- D&C 59:9–10

· ·

PREACH MY GOSPEL

25, 66, 72, 74, 76, 88, 122, 221

· ·

NOTES

Obedience

MUSIC

"Quickly I'll Obey," *Children's Songbook*, 197b
"Keep the Commandments," *Hymns*, no. 303
"How Gentle God's Commands," *Hymns*, no. 125
"Do What Is Right," *Hymns*, no. 237
"Thy Will, O Lord, Be Done," *Hymns*, no. 188

SUMMARY

Because God is our loving Father in Heaven, He knows what is best for our eternal progression and so He gives us commandments to protect us along our earthly journey. In exchange for His guidance, we give Him our obedience. Heavenly Father knows what will make us eternally happy, so commandments are designed to steer us away from things that will harm or destroy us spiritually or physically.

Obedience is a measure of our commitment to God. Obeying out of love is better than out of fear. We can pray for a personal witness that the commandments come from God.

QUOTES

- "The Lord has left no doubt in defining His side and where the Saints should be in their thoughts, words, actions, and practices. We have His counsel in the scriptures and in the words of the prophets." (Joseph B. Wirthlin, "The Lord's Side," *Ensign*, Mar. 1993.)

- "You will need the help of heaven to keep the commandments. You will need it more and more as the days go on. . . . But you can bring the protective powers of heaven down on you by simply deciding to go toward the Savior, to wait on him." (Henry B. Eyring, *To Draw Closer to God,* 1997, 98.)

↝ "The Book of Mormon, in addition to being another testament of Jesus Christ, is a book about the results of keeping and not keeping commandments." (Gregory A. Schwitzer, "Developing Good Judgment and Not Judging Others," *Ensign,* May 2010.)

↝ "My brothers and sisters, the great test of this life is obedience." (Thomas S. Monson, "Obedience Brings Blessings," *Ensign,* May 2013.)

↝ "There is no need for you or for me, in this enlightened age when the fulness of the gospel has been restored, to sail uncharted seas or to travel unmarked roads in search of truth. A loving Heavenly Father has plotted our course and provided an unfailing guide—even obedience. A knowledge of truth and the answers to our greatest questions come to us as we are obedient to the commandments of God." (Thomas S. Monson, "Obedience Brings Blessings," *Ensign,* May 2013.)

* *

GOSPEL ART

Building the Ark (7 GAB)
Abraham Taking Isaac to be Sacrificed (9 GAB)
Joseph Resists Potiphar's Wife (11 GAB)
The Ten Commandments (14 GAB)
Esther (21 GAB)
Daniel Refusing the King's Food and Wine (23 GAB)
Three Men in the Fiery Furnace (25 GAB)
Daniel in the Lions' Den (26 GAB)
Jonah (27 GAB)
John the Baptist Baptizing Jesus (35 GAB)
The Liahona (68 GAB)
Alma Baptizes in the Waters of Mormon (76 GAB)
Two Thousand Young Warriors (80 GAB)
Young Man Being Baptized (103 GAB)
Girl Being Baptized (104 GAB)

* *

VIDEOS

"Obedience to the Ten Commandments": www.lds.org/media-library /video/2015-03-002-obedience-to-the-ten-commandments

"Obedience Brings Blessings": www.lds.org/media-library/video/2014 -06-1130-obedience-brings-blessings

"Abraham and the Sacrifice of Isaac": www.lds.org/media-library/video /2010-12-09-chapter-9-abraham-and-the-sacrifice-of-isaac?category =children/old-testament-stories-friend

"Obedience to the Prophets": www.lds.org/media-library/video/annual -mutual-theme/unit-10-dc

· ·

ARTICLES

↠ Thomas S. Monson, "Obedience Brings Blessings," *Ensign*, May 2013.

↠ L. Tom Perry, "Obedience to Law Is Liberty," *Ensign*, May 2013.

↠ L. Tom Perry, "Obedience through Our Faithfulness," *Ensign*, May 2014.

↠ Robert D. Hales, "If Ye Love Me, Keep My Commandments," May 2014.

↠ M. Russell Ballard, "Learn Obedience and Service," *Ensign*, May 1976.

· ·

OBJECT LESSONS

↠ Ask someone to read the recipe for chocolate chip cookies while you make them. When "oil" is mentioned, add some car oil. When "flour" is read aloud, toss some flowers into the bowl. Add potato chips instead of choco- late chips. Instead of baking soda, toss in some soda pop. Use garlic salt when "salt" is mentioned. Of course, by now the class will be groaning. Talk about how when the Lord asks us to be obedient, we can't pick and choose how we'll interpret the commandments.

↠ Wrap an egg in bubble wrap and tissue and then drop it on the floor. The soft packaging should cushion the egg, which would have broken without the protection. The gospel is designed to protect each of us in the same way—by helping us build layers of testimony as we keep the commandments.

↠ Shine a spotlight on someone. Now ask the volunteer to move one step away. Point out that she may still have a little bit of light on her but not as much as before. Now ask her to move five steps away and show that she no longer has any light on her. The light is Jesus Christ. He is not the one who moves from us. It only takes one step away from the Lord to reduce His light on us. When we sin without repenting, we are taking more and more steps away from Him. To continue to receive the Lord's illumination in our lives, we can't move—we have to stay close to Him and keep the commandments.

CHALLENGE

Consider one of the commandments that you might not be obeying 100 percent. Ponder why the Lord would give such a commandment. How could you be blessed if you followed the commandment with love for the Lord and strict obedience? How would your life be better? How would your spirituality increase? Decide what you will do to improve your commitment to live that particular commandment.

DOCTRINAL MASTERY PASSAGES

- 1 Nephi 3:7
- 2 Nephi 2:27
- 2 Nephi 28:7–9
- Mosiah 4:30
- Alma 37:35
- Exodus 20:3–17
- Joshua 1:8
- Isaiah 29:13–14
- John 7:17
- John 14:15
- 2 Timothy 3:16–17
- James 2:17–18
- D&C 1:37–38
- D&C 14:7
- D&C 58:26–27
- D&C 82:10
- D&C 89:18–21
- D&C 130:18–19
- D&C 130:20–21

PREACH MY GOSPEL

1, 19, 72, 75, 76, 88, 97, 115, 122–26, 150–51, 168–69

NOTES

_____

_____

_____

Prophet

MUSIC

"Come, Listen to a Prophet's Voice," *Hymns*, no. 21
"Come, Sing to the Lord," *Hymns*, no. 10
"God Bless Our Prophet Dear," *Hymns*, no. 24
"Praise to the Man," *Hymns*, no. 27
"We Thank Thee, O God, for a Prophet," *Hymns*, no. 19

SUMMARY

God communicates to His people through a living prophet, a man called through priesthood authority to represent Him. The prophet is also the President of The Church of Jesus Christ of Latter-day Saints and holds the keys of the kingdom on earth. The prophet receives revelation for the Church and leads the administration of priesthood ordinances. He is also called a seer and revelator. By following the Lord's chosen mouthpiece we will never be led astray.

When we sustain the prophet by the show of our raised hand in church, we are not voting for him; we are affirming our support and commitment to follow the Lord's anointed mouthpiece on earth.

QUOTES

- "A prophet is the authorized representative of the Lord. While the world may not recognize him, the important requirement is that God speaks through him." (A. Theodore Tuttle, "What Is a Living Prophet," *Ensign*, July 1973, 18–20.)

- "Sustaining support of prophets, seers, and revelators is not in the upraised hand alone, but more so in our courage, testimony, and faith to listen to, heed, and follow them." (Dennis B. Neuenschwander, "Living Prophets, Seers, and Revelators," *Ensign,* Nov. 2000, 40–42.)
- "When we sustain, it means we *do* something about our belief. Our testimony of the prophet turns into action when we sustain him." (Janette Hales Beckham, "Sustaining the Living Prophets," *Ensign,* May 1996, 84–85.)
- "Surely one of the crowning blessings of membership in this Church is the blessing of being led by living prophets of God." (Kevin R. Duncan, "Our Very Survival," *Ensign,* Nov. 2010.)
- "Prophets often raise a voice of warning, but also provide steady, pragmatic counsel to help us weather the storms of life." (Steven E. Snow, "Get on with Our Lives," *Ensign,* May 2009.)

GOSPEL ART

Building the Ark (7 GAB)
Noah and the Ark with Animals (8 GAB)
Abraham Taking Isaac to Be Sacrificed (9 GAB)
Moses and the Burning Bush (13 GAB)
Boy Samuel Called by the Lord (18 GAB)
Lehi Prophesying to the People of Jerusalem (67 GAB)
Enos Praying (72 GAB)
King Benjamin Addresses His People (74 GAB)
Abinadi before King Noah (75 GAB)
Samuel the Lamanite on the Wall (81 GAB)
The Prophet Joseph Smith (122 GAB)
Latter-day Prophets (122–137 GAB)

VIDEOS

"Follow the Prophet": www.lds.org/manual/preach-my-gospel/asl/chapter3/lesson4
"Life's Greatest Decisions": www.lds.org/media-library/video/2003-09-04-lifes-greatest-decisions
"We Need Living Prophets": www.lds.org/media-library/video/2012-04-15-we-need-living-prophets

"A Steady, Reassuring Voice": www.lds.org/media-library/video/2012-08
-3150-a-steady-reassuring-voice

ARTICLES

F. Michael Watson, "His Servants, the Prophets," *Ensign*, May 2009.
David B. Haight, "A Prophet Chosen of the Lord," *Ensign*, May 1986.
Jeffrey R. Holland, "My Words . . . Never Cease," *Ensign*, May 2008.
Jeffrey R. Holland, "Prophets in the Land Again," *Ensign*, Nov. 2006.
Dieter F. Uchtdorf, "Heeding the Voice of the Prophets," *Ensign*, July 2008.
Gordon B. Hinckley, "We Thank Thee, O God, For A Prophet," *Ensign*, Sept.
1991.

OBJECT LESSONS

- Hold out your fist and ask a volunteer to put his or her hand over yours without actually touching. Challenge him or her to follow your hand's movements up, down, and around. It's pretty hard! Now, have each hand hold onto opposite ends of a pen. See if the volunteer can follow your movements. It's much easier! Explain that the pen represents the prophet. Talk about how following the prophet makes it easier to stay connected to the Savior.

- Tell the class that a coin represents ancient and modern prophets. Ask them which side of the coin is more important. Then ask if the two sides of the coin can be separated. Explain that both sides of the coin work together for the same purpose, just as all prophets throughout the ages have had the common goal of bringing their people to Jesus Christ.

- Invite your class to sign a birthday card for the prophet. You can find out his birthday at www.lds.org.

- Gift wrap two boxes. Leave one empty and put some treats in the other one. Tell the class that one of the boxes has something special in it, while the other one has nothing. Ask a volunteer to choose a box. Let the volunteer see what's inside the box. Ask the class if they want him or her to decide for them. Of course, they'll say yes because she now knows what's in both boxes. We follow the prophet because he has "seen what's in the box" of life! He knows what choices we need to make in order to receive eternal rewards.

- Hold a peanut with the shell in your hand behind your back and tell the class that you're holding something that has never been seen by human eyes before. Of course, they won't believe you. Ask for some volunteers to take a peek and tell the class if what you're saying is true or not. When they testify that you're telling the truth, ask how many believe now that there are witnesses. Some still won't. (They must be nuts.) Talk about how the prophets have "seen" and testify of truth. Some in the world will refuse to believe them . . . will you?

CHALLENGE

Read talks from the most recent general conference to hear what our current prophet and apostles counseled us to do. Make a list of the things you need to work on in your life in order to say you are following the prophet 100 percent.

DOCTRINAL MASTERY PASSAGES

- 1 Nephi 3:7
- Alma 37:6–7
- 3 Nephi 27:27
- Abraham 3:22–23
- Exodus 33:11
- Jeremiah 16:16
- Daniel 2:44–45
- Matthew 16:15–19
- Ephesians 4:11–14
- D&C 84:33–39

PREACH MY GOSPEL

7, 35–36, 44–45, 66, 75, 88

NOTES

_____

_____

_____

_____

_____

Covenants

MUSIC

"Come, We That Love the Lord," *Hymns*, no. 119
"O Love That Glorifies the Son," *Hymns*, no. 295
"God is Love," *Hymns*, no. 87
"Because God Loves Me," *Children's Songbook*, 234
"Seek the Lord Early," *Children's Songbook*, 108
"Keep the Commandments," *Hymns*, no. 303

SUMMARY

Most of us would say that we love God. How do we show Him our sincere love and gratitude? The answer is simple: by doing His will and keeping His commandments (John 14:15). There are two great commandments: to love God and our fellowman. The order of those mandates is significant. If we truly love God, everything else will fall into place in its proper order. The blessings we receive by loving God will help us to love and bless our fellowman.

God desires to bless us, so He makes covenants with us. He shows us that when we obey certain laws of heaven, we receive specific blessings. He is a loving Heavenly Father who made this earth as a school for our learning and progression. We need to believe in God, but also DO His will, despite what others do. We are not only His greatest creation, but we are His sons and daughters. By keeping His commandments and serving others we can become like Him and return to live with Him.

QUOTES

- "True happiness is not made in getting something. True happiness is becoming something. This can be done by being committed to lofty goals. We cannot become something without commitment." (Marvin J. Ashton, "The Word is Commitment," *Ensign*, Oct. 1983.)
- "Love is the measure of our faith, the inspiration for our obedience, and the true altitude of our discipleship." (Dieter F. Uchtdorf, "The Love of God," *Ensign*, Oct. 2009.)
- "To love God with all your heart, soul, mind, and strength is all-consuming and all-encompassing. It is no lukewarm endeavor. It is a total commitment of our very being." (Ezra Taft Benson, "The Great Commandment—Love the Lord," *Ensign*, May 1988.)
- "We have got to reach a higher plane: we have got to love God more than we love the world." (Lorenzo Snow, *Teachings of Presidents of the Church: Lorenzo Snow*, 2011.)

GOSPEL ART

The Brother of Jared Sees the Finger of the Lord (85 GAB)
Three Men in the Fiery Furnace (25 GAB)
Daniel in the Lions' Den (26 GAB)
Abinadi Before King Noah (75 GAB)
Samuel the Lamanite on the Wall (81 GAB)
Joseph Smith in Liberty Jail (97 GAB)
Building the Ark (102 KIT, 7 GAB)
Noah and the Ark with Animals (8 GAB)
Daniel Refusing the King's Meat and Wine (23 GAB)
Calling of the Fishermen (37 GAB)
Christ and the Rich Young Ruler (48 GAB)
Boy Samuel Called by the Lord (18 GAB)
John the Baptist Baptizing Jesus (35 GAB)
Christ Ordaining the Apostles (38 GAB)
Alma Baptizes in the Waters of Mormon (76 GAB)

VIDEOS

"The Two Great Commandments": www.lds.org/media-library/video/2013

-10-1160-the-two-great-commandments (This video features President Ezra Taft Benson!)

"Put God First": www.lds.org/media-library/video/2011-03-019-put-god-first

"I Will Give Myself to Him": www.lds.org/media-library/video/2013-12-1120 -i-will-give-myself-to-him-highlight-3

"Obedience": www.lds.org/media-library/video/2011-03-075-obedience

"The Greatest Commandment": www.lds.org/media-library/video/2011-10 -052-the-greatest-commandment

ARTICLES

- Rex C. Reeve, "Look to God," *Ensign*, Nov. 1982.
- Robert F. Orton, "The First and Great Commandment," *Ensign*, Nov. 2001.
- Dieter F. Uchtdorf, "The Love of God," *Ensign*, Nov. 2009.
- Gordon B. Hinckley, "In These Three I Believe," *Ensign*, July 2006.
- Bernard P. Brockbank, "Knowing God," *Ensign*, July 1972, 121–23.

OBJECT LESSONS

- Show the class a pen. Tell a volunteer, "Try to take pen." When they grab it, say, "No, don't DO it. You were supposed to just TRY." Commitment means we're all in. The Lord takes covenants seriously. We know He will always keep His end of the bargain. He expects us to do the same.
- Begin by showing a padlock and ask what it can be used for. Ask what good a lock is without a key. Discuss how our lives only find meaning in relationship with our Creator. God has made us and this Earth for a purpose. Jesus Christ is the key. Life without God is like a padlock without a key.
- Ask "How many of you would like to see God?" Pass around a mirror and discuss how each one of us is made in His image and how we are truly divine. We can see God's reflection in Jesus. To see God clearly, we need to follow the Savior, follow His example, and serve others. He makes covenants with us so that we can see Him and ourselves more clearly.
- Scramble up the letters to words, using this fun online tool: www.super-kids.com/aweb/tools/words/scramble/. Try words like oancdmemstmn (commandments) or ipisoetrir (priorities). Have the class try to figure out the words. Later, explain that even if we can disguise our true character

from the world, the Lord sees who we really are. Our goal is to become like Him.

- -

CHALLENGE

Create a "To Do" list of things you need to accomplish this week. Put them into two categories: ways you love God and ways you love others. Where are you spending the majority of your time and energy?

- -

DOCTRINAL MASTERY PASSAGES

- 1 Nephi 3:7
- 1 Nephi 19:23
- 2 Nephi 32:3
- Jacob 2:18–19
- Helaman 5:12
- Moroni 7:16–17
- Moroni 10:4–5

- Exodus 20:3–17
- Deut. 7:3–4
- Joshua 24:15
- Job 19:25–26
- Proverbs 3:5–6
- Daniel 2:44–45
- Matthew 6:24

- John 7:17
- John 14:15
- John 17:3
- 2 Thessalonians 2:1–3
- D&C 14:7
- D&C 19:16–19
- D&C 130:20–21

- -

PREACH MY GOSPEL

5, 7, 31–32, 37, 48, 66, 72, 76

- -

NOTES

_____

_____

_____

_____

_____

_____

The Priesthood

MUSIC

"Ye Elders of Israel," *Hymns*, no. 319
"The Priesthood of Our Lord," *Hymns*, no. 320
"Come, All Ye Sons of God," *Hymns*, no. 322
"Rise Up, O Men of God," *Hymns*, no. 323
"See the Mighty Priesthood Gathered," *Hymns*, no. 325
"The Priesthood Is Restored," *Children's Songbook*, 89

SUMMARY

The priesthood is the power and authority of God given to righteous men to enable them to act in God's name for the salvation of the human family. Earthly ordinances, such as baptism, confirmation, administration of the sacrament, and temple sealing ordinances, need to be performed by the correct priesthood authority in order to be valid in the eyes of the Lord. The same power Christ used to create the earth is given to worthy men on it now.

When the Savior established His church during His earthly ministry, He chose humble men to serve as His apostles. When He needed to restore His gospel in latter-days, He did it through a humble young boy. The Lord always looks for the humble in spirit to bear His priesthood and to lead His church. Each of the Twelve Apostles holds all of the priesthood keys on earth; however, only the president of the Church can exercise them in full on behalf of the Church. The united voice of those who hold the keys of the kingdom of God will always guide us to spiritual safety.

Good men and women of all religions are blessed, but without correct divine authority, they cannot receive saving ordinances and attain a celestial glory. As Latter-day Saints, we can inspire priesthood holders around us to honor their priesthood power and use it to bless others' lives.

• •

QUOTES

- "Priesthood is to be used for the benefit of the entire human family, for the upbuilding of men, women, and children alike. There is indeed no privileged class or sex within the true Church of Christ. . . . Men have their work to do and their powers to exercise for the benefit of all the members of the Church. So with woman: Her special gifts are to be exercised for the benefit and uplift of the race" (Quoted by John A. Widtsoe, comp., in *Priesthood and Church Government,* rev. ed. [1954], 92–93.)

- "The man holds the Priesthood, performs the priestly duties of the Church, but his wife enjoys with him every other privilege derived from the possession of the Priesthood. This is made clear, as an example, in the Temple service of the Church. The ordinances of the Temple are distinctly of Priesthood character, yet women have access to all of them, and the highest blessings of the Temple are conferred only upon a man and his wife jointly" (*Priesthood and Church Government* [1965], 83.)

- "Caring for others is the very essence of priesthood responsibility. It is the power to bless, to heal, and to administer the saving ordinances of the gospel." (James E. Faust, "Power of the Priesthood," *Ensign,* May 1997, 41–43.)

- "When we consider how few men who have lived on earth have received the priesthood and how Jesus Christ has empowered those individuals to act in His name, we should feel deeply humble and profoundly grateful for the priesthood we hold." (Richard G. Scott, "Honor the Priesthood and Use It Well," *Ensign,* Nov. 2008, 44–47.)

- "With the priesthood, nothing is impossible in carrying forward the work of the kingdom of God. It is the only power on the earth that reaches beyond the veil of death." (Gordon B. Hinckley, "Priesthood Restoration," *Ensign,* Oct. 1988, 69–72.)

• •

GOSPEL ART

Moses Calls Aaron to the Ministry (15 GAB)
Jacob Blessing His Sons (12 GAB)
Calling of the Fishermen (37 GAB)

Christ Ordaining the Apostles (38 GAB)
Jesus Blessing Jairus's Daughter (41 GAB)
Jesus Washing the Apostles' Feet (55 GAB)
John the Baptist Conferring the Aaronic Priesthood (93 GAB)
Melchizedek Priesthood Restoration (94 GAB)
Baptism (103 GAB)
The Gift of the Holy Ghost (105 GAB)
Blessing the Sacrament (107 GAB)
Passing the Sacrament (108 GAB)
Missionaries Teach the Gospel of Jesus Christ (109–110 GAB)

VIDEOS

"Blessings of the Priesthood": www.lds.org/media-library/video/2009-05
-20-blessings-of-the-priesthood
"Elder Perry on Priesthood, Part 1": www.lds.org/media-library/video/2011
-09-41-elder-perry-on-priesthood-part-1
"Restoration of the Priesthood": www.lds.org/media-library/video/2010-05
-1130-restoration-of-the-priesthood
"Willing and Worthy to Serve": www.lds.org/media-library/video/2012-04
-3060-president-thomas-s-monson
"Let Every Man Learn His Duty: Aaronic Priesthood": www.lds.org/media
-library/video/2010-12-06-let-every-man-learn-his-duty-aaronic
-priesthood
"Becoming a Priesthood Man: Priesthood Duty": www.lds.org/media
-library/video/2010-12-08-becoming-a-priesthood-man-priesthood-duty
"Priesthood and Priesthood Keys—We Are Brothers": www.lds.org
/media-library/video/2012-10-006-priesthood-and-priesthood-keys-we
-are-brothers
"Be Valiant in Courage, Strength, and Activity": www.lds.org/media
-library/video/2012-10-3020-bishop-gary-e-stevenson

ARTICLES

Thomas S. Monson, "Our Sacred Priesthood Trust," *Ensign*, May 2006.
Dallin H. Oaks, "Priesthood Blessings," *Ensign*, May 1987.
Thomas S. Monson, "The Priesthood—A Sacred Gift," *Ensign*, May 2007.
Richard G. Scott, "Honor the Priesthood and Use It Well," *Ensign*, Nov. 2008.

Thomas S. Monson, "True to Our Priesthood Trust," *Ensign*, Nov. 2006.

James E. Faust, "A Royal Priesthood," May 2006, *Ensign*, Nov. 2007.

Henry B. Eyring, "Faith and the Oath and Covenant of the Priesthood," *Ensign*, May 2008.

Thomas S. Monson, "The Priesthood—A Sacred Gift," *Ensign*, May 2007.

OBJECT LESSONS

- Ask someone in the class to hold an umbrella and keep someone in the class dry from the pretend rain that is falling. Note that the umbrella only needs to be held by one person, but both people are kept dry from the rain. So it is with the priesthood; while men can hold the priesthood, it is meant to be used to bless everyone and keep us all protected from the storms of earthly life.

- Show the class a gyroscope. It's not just a toy, but a scientific instrument. To make it work, start spinning it and pull the string. If you put it on a tiny surface it will still spin and stay upright. In fact, whatever the position it's placed in, it will continue to spin. The gyroscope principle is used in a special type of compass used on a ship because the movement won't affect it. There are many things that can knock us off course in life, but if we follow the leadership of the priesthood, our direction will always be right.

- Help the class memorize a part of the oath and covenant of the priesthood in D&C 84. Try some of the memorizing techniques at www.wikihow.com/Memorize.

- Invite someone from each priesthood quorum to share with the sisters what their responsibilities are in serving as a deacon, teacher, priest, elder, and High Priest. You might also invite a Patriarch or Seventy if they're available.

CHALLENGE

Volunteer to drive a deacon to do his fast offering route on the next fast Sunday.

DOCTRINAL MASTERY PASSAGES

- Abraham 3:22–23
- Matthew 16:15–19

- Ephesians 4:11–14
- Hebrews 5:4
- D&C 1:37–38

- D&C 84:33–39
- D&C 121:34–36
- D&C 130:20–21

PREACH MY GOSPEL

32, 37, 83–84, 218

NOTES

_____
_____
_____
_____
_____
_____
_____
_____
_____
_____
_____
_____
_____
_____
_____
_____

Fifth Sunday

Topics Chosen by the Bishopric

Eternal Marriage

MUSIC

"Home Can Be a Heaven on Earth," *Hymns*, no. 298
"I Am a Child of God," *Hymns*, no. 301
"O My Father," *Hymns*, no. 292
"Teach Me to Walk in the Light," *Hymns*, no. 304

SUMMARY

Marriage is ordained of God and is between a man and a woman. Temple marriage is a sacred partnership with God and is essential for exaltation, which is the perfect union of man and woman. Temple marriage is a covenant partnership with the Lord that allows us to seal souls together as eternal families.

Celestial marriage is the crowning ordinance of the gospel of Jesus Christ. The benefits of a temple marriage are not just eternal, but also bless our mortal life together. Joy in marriage grows sweeter as husband and wife both remain faithful and obedient to gospel covenants.

Be sensitive to the brothers and sisters in the class who may have never married, lost a spouse, or divorced. Remind them the Lord has promised a fullness of blessings to all those who are faithful.

QUOTES

◄◦ "To those who keep the covenant of marriage, God promises the fulness of His glory, eternal lives, eternal increase, exaltation in the celestial kingdom, and a fulness of joy." (F. Burton Howard, "Eternal Marriage," *Ensign,* May 2003.)

- "Marriage between a man and a woman is ordained of God, and only through the new and everlasting covenant of marriage can we realize the fullness of all eternal blessings." (David E. Sorensen, "The Honeymoon Trail," *Liahona,* Oct. 1997, 16–19.)
- "Temple marriage is a covenant that bridges death, transcends time, stretches unbreakable into eternity." (Spencer W. Kimball, "First Presidency Message Temples and Eternal Marriage," *Ensign,* Aug. 1974, 2–6.)
- "A successful marriage requires falling in love many times, always with the same person." (Mignon McLaughlin)
- "I am satisfied that a happy marriage is not so much a matter of romance as it is an anxious concern for the comfort and well-being of one's companion." (Gordon B. Hinckley, "What God Hath Joined Together," *Ensign,* May 1991.)

GOSPEL ART

Adam and Eve Kneeling at an Altar (4 GAB)
Adam and Eve Teaching Their Children (4 GAB)
Jacob Blessing His Sons (12 GAB)
Lehi's Dream (69 GAB)
Elijah Appearing in the Kirtland Temple (95 GAB)
Young Couple Going to the Temple (120 GAB)

VIDEO

"Eternal Marriage": https://www.lds.org/manual/preach-my-gospel/asl/chapter3/lesson5#eternal-marriage

ARTICLES

Spencer W. Kimball, "The Importance of Celestial Marriage," *Ensign,* Oct. 1979, 2–6.
Bruce C. Hafen, "Covenant Marriage," *Ensign,* Nov. 1996, 26–28.
F. Burton Howard, "Eternal Marriage," *Ensign,* May 2003, 92–94.
Spencer W. Kimball, "Temples and Eternal Marriage," *Ensign,* Aug. 1974, 2–6.
Marion D. Hanks, "Eternal Marriage," *Ensign,* Nov. 1984.

L. Whitney Clayton, "Marriage: Watch and Learn," *Ensign*, May 2013.

· ·

OBJECT LESSONS

⚬ Have two volunteers hold a short string across the front the room, one on each end. Now ask another volunteer to attach a clothespin to the string, except only give him or her half of a clothespin. The third volunteer obviously won't be able to attach it. Give them a complete clothespin and allow him or her to attach it to the string. Now ask another volunteer to cut the string with scissors; however, only give them one half of the scissors. Obviously, they won't be able to complete the task. Now give them a real pair of scissors and allow them to cut the string.

Both items serve as great analogies for marriage. If only one person is trying to hang on, it won't work; you need both partners to work together. Likewise, if both partners in the marriage choose "cutting" remarks and are always fighting, it won't take long for everything to fall apart.

⚬ Have a husband and wife play pretend tug-of-war, using a paper chain. The chain represents civil marriage. It doesn't take long to separate if husband and wife are pulling at opposite ends with different goals. If the chain isn't strong, it won't take much for it to break. Now ask the same husband and wife play tug-of-war, this time using a metal chain, which represents temple marriage. With a strong foundation, even if the couple struggles through life they can hold the marriage together.

⚬ Hold up a donut and compare it to temporal marriage: sweet and delicious, but built around a big hole: "'til death do us part." Tell the sisters and brothers, "do-nut settle for a marriage that won't last into the eternities." Pass around cinnamon rolls, comparing those to eternal marriage without a hole.

· ·

CHALLENGE

If you are married, write a list of all the good qualities you see in your spouse. Refer to this list when you get frustrated with him or her! Choose one new act of service you will perform for him or her this week that you've never done before. Plan your next date night.

If you have never been married, pray for patience. Look online for a Singles Conference you could attend and invite some friends you could attend it with. If you are an older widow or widower, pray for comfort until you and your spouse can be reunited. Discover ways you can use your talents to bless others.

· ·

DOCTRINAL MASTERY PASSAGES

- 2 Nephi 2:25
- Moses 1:39
- Genesis 1:26–27
- Genesis 39:9
- Exodus 20:3–17
- Deuteronomy 7:3–4
- 2 Timothy 3:1–5
- D&C 131:1–4
- D&C 137:7–10

· ·

PREACH MY GOSPEL

3, 31, 47-50, 54, 85-86, 159, 164–65

· ·

NOTES

_____

_____

_____

_____

_____

_____

_____

_____

_____

_____

_____

_____

_____

Repentance

MUSIC

"Repentance," *Children's Songbook*, 98
"Help Me, Dear Father," *Children's Songbook*, 99
"With Humble Heart," *Hymns*, no. 171
"Savior, Redeemer of My Soul," *Hymns*, no. 112
"Come Unto Jesus," *Hymns*, no. 117

SUMMARY

The first principle of the gospel is faith in the Lord Jesus Christ and the second is repentance. Faith is a principle of action that compels us to repent and be obedient.

Repentance is essential to our salvation and exaltation. We all sin when we are less than perfect in our obedience to God's laws. Only Jesus Christ was without sin. A merciful Father in Heaven sent His Son to atone for our sins in order that we may return to His presence.

Repentance is the process that allows us to receive forgiveness and grow spiritually. The steps of repentance include recognizing our error, feeling sorrow for our sin, forsaking our bad behavior, confessing our sins to the Lord's servant, and making restitution to right the wrong. We are also commanded to forgive others, to not procrastinate our repentance, and to raise a voice of warning to the world.

QUOTES

⟶ "No part of walking by faith is more difficult than walking the road of repentance. However, with 'faith unto repentance,' we can push road-blocks out of the way, moving forward to beg God for mercy." (Neal A. Maxwell, "Repentance," *Ensign*, Nov. 1991.)

‣ "The promise of the Lord is that He will cleanse our garments with His blood. . . . He can redeem us from our personal fall." (Lynn A. Mickelsen, "The Atonement, Repentance, and Dirty Linen," *Ensign,* Nov. 2003.)

‣ "The steps of repentance . . . produce purity, peace of mind, self-respect, hope, and finally, a new person with a renewed life and abundance of opportunity." (Richard G. Scott, "Finding Forgiveness," *Ensign,* May 1995, 75–77.)

‣ "Repentance is timeless. The evidence of repentance is transformation." (Spencer W. Kimball, "What Is True Repentance," *New Era,* May 1974, 4–7.)

‣ "What a wonderful gift the Savior offers—to feel the joy of being free from sin." (Neil L. Andersen, "Clean Again!" *New Era,* Apr. 1997, 4–7.

GOSPEL ART

Jesus Praying in Gethsemane (56 GAB)
The Crucifixion (57 GAB)
Jesus at the Door (65 GAB)
Jesus the Christ (1 GAB)
Enos Praying (72 GAB)
Conversion of Alma the Younger (77 GAB)
The Ten Commandments (14 GAB)
Abraham Taking Isaac to Be Sacrificed (9 GAB)
Three Men in the Fiery Furnace (25 GAB)
Daniel in the Lions' Den (26 GAB)
Moses and the Brass Serpent (16 GAB)
Christ Healing a Blind Man (42 GAB)
Jesus Blessing Jairus's Daughter (41 GAB)
Two Thousand Young Warriors (80 GAB)
The Brother of Jared Sees the Finger of the Lord (85 GAB)

VIDEOS

"Cleansing the Inner Vessel": www.lds.org/media-library/video/2010-10 -4020-president-boyd-k-packer

"Replace Suffering with Joy": www.lds.org/media-library/video/2012-08
-2320-replace-suffering-with-joy

"Repentance Leads Us to Christ's Grace": www.lds.org/media-library
/video/2012-08-2695-repentance-leads-us-to-christs-grace-1

"Repentance and Change": www.lds.org/general-conference/2003/10
/repentance-and-change&query=repentence

"Waiting on Our Road to Damascus": www.lds.org/general-conference/2011
/04/waiting-on-the-road-to-damascus

ARTICLES

Spencer W. Kimball, "The Gospel of Repentance," *Ensign*, Oct. 1982.
Ezra Taft Benson, "Cleansing the Inner Vessel," *Ensign*, May 1986.
Boyd K. Packer, "I Will Remember Your Sins No More," *Ensign*, May 2006.
Russell M. Nelson, "Jesus Christ—the Master Healer," *Ensign*, Nov. 2005.
David A. Bednar, "Clean Hands and a Pure Heart," *Ensign*, Nov. 2007.

OBJECT LESSONS

- Hand out various objects to class members and have them explain how those items are like repentance. Easy objects to use include:

    » soap
    » pencil eraser
    » knotted rope
    » calculator
    » sponge

- Start with a jar filled with clear water and label it "US." Next, take food coloring, labeled "SIN," and add a drop each time you discuss various sins. Talk about the Atonement as you pour some bleach, labeled "ATONE-MENT" into the jar. Stir the water, which represents REPENTANCE. The class should see that the water clears up and is "clean" like before.

- Wear a long-sleeved white buttoned-up shirt that has holes in it, dirt marks, food smears and words that say things like: drugs, profanity, gossip, anger, stealing, lying, disobedience, etc. When you talk about repentance, take that shirt off, revealing a clean, white shirt underneath.

- Show the class a pepper shaker and explain that the pepper represents temptations. Shake some of the pepper into a dish with water in it. Read

D&C 10:5 and ask the class what we should do when we're tempted. Now show the class a bar of soap and explain that it represents prayer. Invite a volunteer to rub his or her fingers on the bar of soap and then touch the surface of the water in the dish. (The pepper will move to the sides of the dish.) Brigham Young once said, "Prayer keeps a man from sin, and sin keeps a man from prayer."

• •

CHALLENGE

When we partake of the sacrament, we should reflect on Christ's Atonement, recommitting ourselves to do better each week. Set a goal to work on one specific Christlike quality you will work on this week. Repent from something today that you're currently struggling with.

• •

DOCTRINAL MASTERY PASSAGES

- 2 Nephi 2:27
- 2 Nephi 28:7–9
- Mosiah 4:30
- Alma 32:21
- Alma 34:32–34
- Alma 41:10
- Ether 12:6
- Genesis 39:9
- Exodus 20:3–17
- Psalms 24:3–4
- Proverbs 3:5–6
- Isaiah 1:18
- Isaiah 55:8–9
- John 14:15
- James 1:5–6
- James 2:17–18
- D&C 19:16–19
- D&C 58:42–43
- D&C 59:9–10
- D&C 82:3

• •

PREACH MY GOSPEL

49–50, 62–63, 93–95, 155, 187–90, 195

• •

NOTES

_____

_____

_____

_____

Temple Blessings

MUSIC

"God Is in His Holy Temple," *Hymns*, no. 132
"High on the Mountain Top," *Hymns*, no. 5
"Holy Temples on Mount Zion," *Hymns*, no. 289
"How Beautiful Thy Temples, Lord," *Hymns*, no. 288
"We Love Thy House, O God," *Hymns*, no. 247

SUMMARY

Sacred temples are built as a school for the Saints to receive eternal ordinances, make important covenants, and gain vital knowledge that will bind their families together forever and allow them to enter into the celestial kingdom. Attending the temple is a symbol of our faithful membership in the Church. Prophets have encouraged us to get a temple recommend and use it as often as we can. Being "temple worthy," even when we don't live near a temple will allow us to become more like the Savior in thought and deed.

The blessings that are received are on both sides of the veil! Our dead ancestors can receive saving ordinances and we can serve as "Saviors on Mount Zion." We need each other. Temples are truly designed to bind heaven and earth.

QUOTES

- "I think there is no place in the world where I feel closer to the Lord than in one of His holy temples." (Thomas S. Monson, "Blessings of the Temple," *Ensign*, Oct. 2010.)
- "Attending the temple gives us a clearer perspective and a sense of purpose

and peace." (Thomas S. Monson, "Blessings of the Temple," *Ensign*, Oct. 2010.)

- "It is a place of peace, solitude, and inspiration. Regular attendance will enrich your life with greater purpose. It will permit you to provide deceased ancestors the exalting ordinances you have received. Go to the temple. You know it is the right thing to do. Do it now." (Richard G. Scott, "Receive the Blessings of the Temple," *Ensign*, May 1999.)

- "The Lord's work is one majestic work focused upon hearts, covenants, and priesthood ordinances." (David A. Bednar, "Missionary, Family History, and Temple Work," *Ensign*, Oct. 2014.)

- "Always prayerfully express gratitude for the incomparable blessings that flow from temple ordinances. Live each day so as to give evidence to Father in Heaven and His Beloved Son of how very much those blessings mean to you." (Richard G. Scott, "How Can We Make the Most of Temple Attendance?" *Ensign*, Mar. 2012.)

- "When a temple is conveniently nearby, small things may interrupt your plans to go to the temple. Set specific goals, considering your circumstances, of when you can and will participate in temple ordinances. Then, do not allow anything to interfere with that plan. This pattern will guarantee that those who live in the shadow of the temple will be as blessed as are those who plan far ahead and make a long trip to the temple." (Richard G. Scott, "How Can We Make the Most of Temple Attendance?" *Ensign*, Mar. 2012.)

- -

GOSPEL ART

Jesus Christ (1 GAB)
Boy Jesus in the Temple (34 GAB)
Jesus Cleansing the Temple (51 GAB)
My Father's House (52 GAB)
Melchizedek Priesthood Restoration (94 GAB)
Elijah Appearing in the Kirtland Temple (95 GAB)
Kirtland Temple (117 GAB)
Nauvoo Illinois Temple (118 GAB)
Salt Lake Temple (119 GAB)
Young Couple Going to the Temple (120 GAB)
Temple Baptismal Font (121 GAB)
Nauvoo Temple (118 GAB)

VIDEOS

"To Have Peace and Happiness": www.lds.org/media-library/video/2010-09
-0040-to-have-peace-and-happiness

"Why Mormons Build Temples": www.lds.org/media-library/video/2010-05
-1210-why-mormons-build-temples

"Temples are a Beacon": www.lds.org/media-library/video/2012-01-002
-temples-are-a-beacon

"The Blessings of the Temple": www.lds.org/media-library/video/2009
-03-10-the-blessings-of-the-temple

ARTICLES

Russell M. Nelson, "Prepare for Blessings of the Temple," *Ensign*, March
2002, 17.

David E. Sorensen, "The Doctrine of Temple Work," *Ensign*, Oct. 2002, 30.

Howard W. Hunter, "A Temple-Motivated People," *Ensign,* Feb. 1995.

Stacy Vickery, "Temple Blessings Now and Eternally," *Ensign*, Sept. 2011.

Richard G. Scott, "Receive the Temple Blessings," *Ensign,* May 1999.

Howard W. Hunter, "We Have A Work To Do," *Ensign*, Mar. 1995, 64–65.

Dennis B. Neuenschwander, *"Bridges and Eternal Keepsakes," Ensign*, May
1999, 83–85.

Gerrit W. Gong, "Temple Mirrors of Eternity: A Testimony of Family,"
Ensign, Nov. 2010.

OBJECT LESSONS

↝ Show the class several items (or pictures of items): candy, coins, $20 bill,
stuffed animal, diamond ring. Ask the class which item they think a baby
would be most interested in. (Candy and toy.) Ask why the baby wouldn't
select the most expensive item? (She doesn't understand the value of it.)
Talk about how some people don't understand the value of temples, so
they make choices that might prevent them from being worthy to enter
the temple.

↝ Invite the sisters and brothers to share pictures of their favorite temple and
share faith-promoting stories about how the temple has blessed their lives.

↝ Access the internet in your building and find some of the newer temples under construction or remodeling by visiting them via Google Earth and Street Maps!

- ➻ Invite someone in your ward who has recently attended the temple for the first time to talk about how they prepared and how their experience made them feel closer to the Savior. You can also invite some of the youth to share their experiences about going to the temple to do temple baptisms.

CHALLENGE

Hang a picture of the temple in your home. Attend the temple preparation class if your ward or branch offers it. Renew your temple recommend (if it has expired) and keep it in your wallet. Choose your family's next vacation destination based on which temple you would like to visit!

DOCTRINAL MASTERY PASSAGES

- Job 19:25–26
- 1 Corinthians 15:20–22
- 1 Corinthians 15:29
- D&C 131:1–4
- D&C 137:7–10

PREACH MY GOSPEL

31–32, 47–50, 52–54, 85–86, 159–65

NOTES

_____

_____

_____

_____

_____

_____

Virtue

MUSIC

"Glorious Things Are Sung of Zion," *Hymns*, no. 48
"Today, While the Sun Shines," *Hymns*, no. 229
"If You Could Hie to Kolob," *Hymns*, no. 284
"Go, Ye Messengers of Glory," *Hymns*, no. 262

SUMMARY

We only get one body; therefore, we must nurture and protect it. It houses our spirit and reveals our self-mastery and obedience. When we cling to virtue, our bodies and spirits glow with peace, happiness, and confidence before the Lord. We need to embrace all that is good and virtuous in the world so that there is no room in our lives for that which is evil and immoral.

We need to continually call upon the Lord for both mental and physical strength to resist the temptations and filth that the world offers. If we succumb to sin, we can be forgiven through sincere repentance and the Atonement of Jesus Christ.

Virtue isn't just resisting evil; it's about spreading light in a dark world. The world is desperate for truth and light. It is our opportunity to be the light, as well as hold up the Savior's light.

QUOTES

- "Virtue consists, not in abstaining from vice, but in not desiring it." (George Bernard Shaw)
- "I know of nothing that will qualify us for the constant companionship

of the Holy Ghost as much as virtue." (Linda S. Reeves, "Worthy of Our Promised Blessings," *Ensign,* Nov. 2015.)

- "My earnest prayer is that you will have the courage required to refrain from judging others, the courage to be chaste and virtuous, and the courage to stand firm for truth and righteousness." (Thomas S. Monson, "May You Have Courage," *Ensign*, May 2009.)

- "Now is the time for each of us to arise and unfurl a banner to the world calling for a return to virtue." (Elaine S. Dalton, "A Return to Virtue," *Ensign*, Nov. 2008.)

- "You must be guardians of virtue. The Young Women values are Christlike attributes which imbue the value of virtue. We now call upon you to join with us in leading the world in a return to virtue. In order to do so, you must practice virtue and holiness by eliminating from your life anything that is evil." (Elaine S. Dalton, "Love Her Mother," *Ensign*, Nov. 2011.)

GOSPEL ART

Adam and Eve Kneeling at an Altar (4 GAB)
Adam and Eve Teaching Their Children (5 GAB)
City of Zion is Taken Up (6 GAB)
Joseph Resists Potiphar's Wife (11 GAB)
Daniel Refusing the King's Food and Wine (23 GAB)
Mary and Martha (45 GAB)
Mary and the Resurrected Jesus Christ (59 GAB)
Jesus Washing the Apostles' Feet (55 GAB)
Jesus Cleansing the Temple (51 GAB)
Joseph Smith Seeks Wisdom in the Bible (89 GAB)
Young Couple Going to the Temple (120 GAB)

VIDEOS

"A Return to Virtue": www.lds.org/general-conference/2008/10/a-return-to
-virtue
"Virtue: For Such a Time as This": www.lds.org/media-library/video/2009
-05-18-virtue-for-such-a-time-as-this
"Virtue": www.lds.org/media-library/video/topics/virtue
"Virtuous Young Women": www.lds.org/media-library/video/2011-12-09

-virtuous-young-women?category=standards-standards/dress-and
-appearance-standards

"Guardians of Virtue—We Believe in Being Chaste": www.lds.org/media
-library/video/topics/chastity

"Dress and Appearance": www.lds.org/media-library/video/standards
-standards/dress-and-appearance-standards

ARTICLES

Elaine S. Dalton, "A Return to Virtue," *Ensign*, Oct. 2008.
Thomas S. Monson, "May You Have Courage" *Ensign*, May 2009.
Jeffrey R. Holland, "Personal Purity" *Ensign*, Nov. 1999.
Neal A. Maxwell, "Reasons to Stay Pure," *New Era*, March 2003.
H. David Burton, "Let Virtue Garnish Your Thoughts," *Ensign*, Nov. 2009.
Mary N. Cook, "A Virtuous Life—Step by Step," *Ensign*, May 2009.
D. Todd Christofferson, "Moral Discipline," *Ensign*, Nov. 2009.

OBJECT LESSONS

- ↪ During the lesson, invite one of the sisters or brothers to DRAW your lesson on the chalkboard. In other words, they illustrate what they hear the class talk about. You can rotate other students as artists every five minutes. It's always fun and entertaining to see what they draw!
- ↪ Before the lesson, take pictures of as many students as you can participating in some kind of virtuous activity to show all of the good things your ward is doing in your community.
- ↪ Divide the class into small groups and invite them to write a parable about something virtuous.
- ↪ Invite the Young Women to come in and share a message about virtue. It is one of their Young Women values that is emphasized in the Church.

CHALLENGE

Walk around your home and evaluate what is "virtuous, lovely, or of good report or praiseworthy" and what is not. Remove items and habits that draw you away from the spirit of the Lord. Do you have a picture of the temple or the Savior in your home? Are scriptures readily available on a bookshelf or nightstand? Could neighbors see that you believe in Christ if they walked into your home?

. . . .

DOCTRINAL MASTERY PASSAGES

- 2 Nephi 9:28–29
- Jacob 2:18–19
- Mosiah 3:19
- Ether 12:27
- Moroni 7:45

- Moses 7:18
- Psalms 24:3–4
- 1 Corinthians 10:13
- 2 Timothy 3:1–5
- 2 Timothy 3:16–17

- D&C 58:26–27
- D&C 64:9–11
- D&C 88:123–24
- D&C 89:18–21

. . . .

PREACH MY GOSPEL

77, 87, 90, 91, 115, 118, 123–26, 168, 169

. . . .

NOTES

_____

_____

_____

_____

_____

_____

_____

_____

_____

_____

_____

_____

Website Resources

No need to reinvent the wheel, especially when you're using that wheel to drive on the Information Super Highway! The internet has an endless resource of ideas, recipes, downloads, crafts, lesson material, music, and instructions for almost anything you'd like to do in your Relief Society or Priesthood Quorum Sunday lessons.

Allow me to give you a serious word of caution about doing online searches. If you enter "Women" into a search engine you will get suggestions for links to all kinds of horrible pornographic websites. You must type in "LDS Women" or "Relief Society," and even then, look at the description of the site before you click on it!

• •

LDS WEBSITE RESOURCES

- www.lds.org (The official website of The Church of Jesus Christ of Latter-day Saints. This should be your first stop on the Web.)
- www.jennysmith.net
- www.theideadoor.com
- www.mormon.org
- www.mormonhub.com
- www.mormonfind.com
- www.lightplanet.com/mormons
- www.JeanniGould.com
- www.sugardoodle.net
- www.ldssplash.com
- www.ldstoday.com

MERCHANDISE

- www.ldscatalog.com (Church distribution center to order materials)

- www.byubookstore.com
- www.ldsliving.com
- www.deseretbook.com
- www.ctr-ring.com

LDS RELIEF SOCIETY BLOGS

- enrichmentideas.blogspot.com
- thereliefsocietyblog.blogspot.com
- www.hollyscorner.com/blog/lds-resources/relief-society
- www.mormonmomma.com/index.php/category/church/relief-society
- lds.families.com/blog/category/1071
- segullah.org/daily-special/putting-the-relief-in-relief-society
- feastuponthewordblog.org
- happyjellybeans.blogspot.com

INTERNET GROUPS

I highly recommend that you join a Yahoo Group. It's free to join and you'll meet some of the nicest people around! People share helpful ideas and tips in a real-time setting. You can receive the emails individually or as a daily digest. Some groups are more active than others so the quantity of emails will vary. No reason to reinvent the wheel when another great Relief Society teacher has already done it out there somewhere!

- groups.yahoo.com/group/ReliefSociety-L
- uk.groups.yahoo.com/group/Relief_SocietyLDS
- groups.yahoo.com/group/ldsreliefsocietypresidency
- groups.yahoo.com/group/LDSReliefSocietyMeetings

CLIP ART

I'm thankful for talented artists who share their wonderful creations with me, since I have trouble drawing decent stick people! Here are some of those generous artists:

Most of the websites mentioned above, plus the following:

- www.christysclipart.com
- www.graphicgarden.com
- designca.com/lds
- www.coloringbookfun.com
- www.stums.org/closet/html/index.html

- www.oneil.com.au/lds/pictures.html
- lds.about.com/library/gallery/clipart/blclipart_gallery_subindex.htm
- www.clipart.com
- www.coloring.ws/coloring.html
- www.apples4theteacher.com

MUSIC

- www.lds.org/music
- www.mormonchannel.org
- www.lds.org/youth/music
- www.defordmusic.com
- lds.about.com/library/clipart/blnewera_music_1975.htm (Great index of all sheet music offered in the New Era & Ensign magazines from 1975 to 1989.)
- www.mormonhaven.com/music.htm
- www.ldsmusictoday.com
- www.ldsmusicsource.com
- www.ldspianosolo.com
- www.deseretbook.com/LDS-Music/Sheet-Music-Downloads/s/1395

Extra Notes

EXTRA NOTES

About the Author

Trina Boice grew up in California and currently lives in Las Vegas where she teaches at the famous Le Cordon Bleu College for Culinary Arts. You can see her yummy food pictures on Instagram! She is also a professor at BYU-Idaho where she teaches the international students in the inspiring Pathway program online.

In 2004 she was honored as the California Young Mother of the Year, an award which completely amuses her four sons. Trina is currently a doctoral student at CTU and also studied at the University of Salamanca in Spain, later returning there to serve an LDS mission in Madrid for 1.5 years. She has a Real Estate license, travel agent license, two master's degrees, and a black belt in Tae Kwon Do, although she's the first one to admit she'd pass out from fright if she were ever really attacked by a bad guy.

She earned two bachelor's degrees from BYU where she competed on the speech and debate team and the ballroom dance team. She was president of the National Honor Society Phi Eta Sigma and served as ASBYU Secretary of Student Community Services.

She worked as a legislative assistant for a Congressman in Washington, DC, and was given the "Points of Light" Award and Presidential Volunteer Service Award for her domestic and international community service. She wrote a column called "The Boice Box" for a newspaper in Georgia, where she lived for fifteen years. She taught Spanish at a private high school and ran an appraisal business with her husband for twenty years. She currently writes for several newspapers and websites.

Trina was selected by KPBS in San Diego to be a political correspondent during the last presidential election. If she told you what she really did, she'd have to kill you.

A popular and entertaining speaker, Trina is the author of twenty-three books with another one hitting stores soon! You can read more about her books and upcoming events at www.TrinasBooks.com.

Check out her Mormon Mom movie reviews at www.MovieReviewMom.com and author web site at www.TrinasBooks.com.

Scan to visit

www.TrinasBooks.com